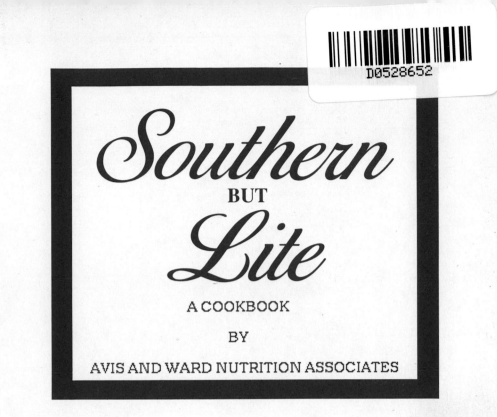

Southern

BUT

Lite

A COOKBOOK

BY

AVIS AND WARD NUTRITION ASSOCIATES

Copies may be obtained from:

Avis and Ward Nutrition, Inc.
200 Professional Drive
West Monroe, LA. 71291

First printing   October, 1989   -   3,000
Second printing   February, 1990   -   3,000
Third printing   August, 1990   -   5,000
Fourth printing   June, 1991   -   5,000
Copyright   1989

ISBN: 0-9628683-0-2

Printed in the USA by
WIMMER BROTHERS
A Wimmer Company
Memphis • Dallas

James L Kendrick, III was born in Shreveport, Louisiana. At a early age, he was inspired by watching the artists on Jackson Square in New Orleans. James Kendrick is a self-taught, full-time artist of 14 years. He studied at the University of Southwestern in Lafayette, Louisiana and is a Vietnam veteran.

The painting by James L Kendrick, III shown on the cover is available as Limited Edition Print series. For information on this and other prints by Mr. Kendrick, contact:

Kendrick III Studio
34 Moselle Drive
Kenner, Louisiana   70065

Colleen Cline Johnson is a free lance artist who lives in Monroe, Louisiana. She has a business, Southern Exposure Note Cards and Prints, which features pen and ink drawings of Southern subject matter, as seen on the dividers throughout the book. Colleen has studied art at five (5) university settings in the United States and abroad. She currently is teaching art to elementary and middle school students.

ACKNOWLEDGMENTS

We want to thank all the people
who have made this book possible
and those who have shared their
traditional southern recipes.

Billie Duffie
Annette Berry
Family and Friends

Nutritional management as well as exercise management are major modalities in treatment of the majority of diseases seen in general practice. Without excellent nutritional information, all of the other modalities of treatment are generally to no avail in the management of these diseases. These include disease from diabetes to hypertension.

Clyde E. Elliott, M.D.
Family Practice

The most recent ADA guidelines stress the importance of a low-fat high fiber diet in reducing the vascular complications of diabetes and improving blood sugar control.

Robert Ewing, M.D.
Internal Medicine

I feel my patients benefit from individualized nutritional counseling and low-fat recipes offering alternatives to traditional southern cooking.

Ronald Hammett ,M.D.   Donald Hammett, M.D.
Pulmonary Medicine   Internal Medicine

The recipes used in the Avis and Ward program have helped my clients make permanent lifestyle changes leading to better cardiovascular health.

Dr. Ronald Keopke, M.D.
Cardiologist

This is the best cookbook to reduce fat and sodium without sacrificing good southern flavor.

Mayor Dave Norris
West Monroe, LA

The Avis and Ward approach to a low-fat high fiber diet has served as an invaluable tool in the treatment of cardiovascular disease.

William D. Smith M.D.
Cardiologist

TABLE OF CONTENTS

INTRODUCTION

For almost ten years, we have been working with individuals in private nutritional counseling practice.

The medical community has recognized for some time the importance of good nutrition and lifestyle changes as a preventative medicine. However, it still amazes us to see so much misinformation. With all the weight control clinics, fad diets, and prepackaged foods, the public stays in a constant state of confusion.

The Registered Licensed Dietitian is the qualified nutrition expert, educated and trained in that profession. We do not diagnose a patient; however, we feel we compliment a physician's care of that patient. Today, more than ever, there is a need to practice good nutrition. Now an individual can lower risk of certain cancers, hypertension, diabetes, and coronary artery disease. For this reason in our clinic, we saw a need for a simple straightforward book offering the layman sound advice and information for improving overall nutrition and eating habits.

Whether you wish to lower your cholesterol, you want to lose weight, or simply wish to practice good nutrition, we have combined guidelines and recipes to help you take responsibility for your health.

We hope this book will allow you to start making some of those changes and living a quality life.

OUR APPROACH

Our approach to weight loss and good nutrition needs to be a practical one. The changes made to improve eating habits have to be permanent for longterm success. It's best to make a compromise of your normal eating habits and make changes you can live with, not just to lose weight, but to keep it off. A registered dietitian can assist you in the assessment of your nutritional status.

Setting an ideal weight is not always as easy as glancing at a height and weight chart. Height and weight charts provide only a general indicator. These tables were developed by life insurance companies from statistics of adults who were already overweight. It does, however, give recommended body weights.

Much of a person's ideal weight depends on an individual's structure. Individuals who are athletic may be overweight by the charts but have very little body fat. Some people may be in the ideal body range, but have a large percentage of their body in fat.

Lean body mass must be considered in setting a target goal weight. Preservation of lean body mass must be considered to avoid wasting away of muscle tissues. People who have dieted by crashing pounds off lose lean muscle mass. This can be dangerous depending on the site of muscle lost and, over a period of time, an individual can deplete muscle mass to a point of increasing the percentage of fat tissue until it is greater than muscle tissue.

An individual's muscle tissue burns more calories than the fat tissue in terms of BMR (Basal Metabolic Rate). BMR, in layman's terms, is simply the number of calories needed to maintain your bodily functions and energy level at rest. If you take in calories in excess of what is needed and do not exercise, you will gain weight. When dieting, caution also has to be taken not to lower the calories so low that the body lowers the BMR to adapt to the new conditions. This is one of the reasons people who have dieted a good deal, generally without exercise, gain weight more easily and lose with greater difficulty.

Exercise plays a vital role in losing weight. Increased physical activity can promote weight loss and decrease body stores of fat. Lean body mass is preserved and increased when exercise and diet are combined.

Low intensity and long duration activities are recommended to optimize fat loss and retain muscle mass while dieting. A physician should be consulted before beginning any exercise program. We recommend exercise no less than three (3) times per week but five (5) times, if possible, while trying to lose weight.

Again, a practical approach must be taken to exercise. Like diet behavior changes, exercise has to be lifelong, too. In choosing an exercise program, think about what you will and can do. Walking is the most practical choice for most people. A walking program is inexpensive to get into and causes little stress on an individual's system.

After establishing your ideal body weight and exercise program, attention has to be given to changing eating habits.

WHAT DO THE RECIPES TELL YOU?

Each recipe lists: Calories
        Cholesterol
        Saturated Fat-SF
        Sodium
        Protein-PRO
        Carbohydrates-CHO
        Fat
        Exchanges
        Yield
        Servings

Nutrient variations occur using various sources of data. The United States government publication <u>Nutritive Value of Foods, Bowes and Church's Food Values of Portions Commonly Used</u>, and the Nutritionist III software program were used for recipe calculations. The nutrient information was averaged when variances occurred to obtain the most precise data. Exchange information was computed with the Nutritionist III software and by hand calculations. Exchanges were rounded off in many cases for ease of use. Meat exchanges and milk exchanges were shown as lean meat and skim milk, with remaining grams of fat shown in fat exchanges.

1 oz lean meat	=	3	gms fat
1 oz. med. fat meat	=	5	gms fat
1 oz. high fat meat	=	8	gms fat
1 cup skim milk	=	0	gms fat
1 cup 2% milk	=	5	gms fat
1 cup whole milk	=	10	gms fat

Many dessert recipes contain refined white sugar. We recommend consulting a registered dietitian before using these recipes for diabetes. Normally, in our clinic, we virtually eliminate refined white sugar when counseling with diabetics and many weight control problems. The chapter entitled Traditional Southern Foods has been used an educational tool. It illustrates many of the typical southern foods and the high fat foods we consume in the south.

Otherwise, all other recipes are excellent for diabetics, heart patients, and health conscious families.

Your meal plan should be individualized, taking into consideration your height, present weight, ideal weight, sex, activity, health status, and medications.

Appetizers
and
Beverages

ARTICHOKE BALLS

2 cloves garlic, minced
1/2 teaspoon onion, minced
2 tablespoons olive oil
16 oz. artichoke hearts
1/4 cup eggbeaters
1/2 cup seasoned bread crumbs
1/2 cup parmesan cheese, grated

Saute' garlic and onion in oil. Drain and mash artichokes. Add artichokes, eggbeaters, garlic, and onions. Cook 5 minutes, stirring constantly. Set aside and allow to cook a little. In another dish, mix cheese and bread crumbs. Roll the warm mixture into balls and coat with the dry mixture. Chill in refrigerator several hours. Serve cold.

Yield: 4 dozen small balls

Calories: 42 per 2 artichoke balls
Exchanges: 1 Vegetable
             1/2 Fat

Cholesterol: less than 1 Mg   PRO: 2 Gm
SF: less than 1 Gm   CHO: 4 Gm
Sodium: 34 Mg   Fat: 2 Gm

BROCCOLI CHEESE SQUARES

2 (10 oz.) packages chopped frozen broccoli
3/4 cup egg substitute
1 cup 2% milk
1 cup flour
1 teaspoon baking powder
1 teaspoon salt
8 oz. grated low-fat cheddar cheese
2 tablespoons chopped onion
Butter flavored cooking spray

Preheat oven to 350 degrees. Spray 13 x 9 x 2-inch pan with cooking spray. Thaw broccoli and press dry. Beat egg substitute and milk until frothy. Blend flour, baking powder, and salt. Stir into egg mixture, mixing well. Fold in broccoli, onion, and cheese. Spoon into baking pan; spread evenly. Baking about 35 minutes or until set. Let stand 5 minutes before cutting.

Yield: 4 dozen squares

Calories: 38 per square
Exchanges: 1 Vegetable

Cholesterol: 4 Mg   PRO: 2 Gm
SF: 1 Gm   CHO: 3 Gm
Sodium: 35 Mg   Fat: 2 Gm

COCKTAIL MEATBALLS

1 pound ground turkey
2 tablespoons seasoned bread crumbs
1 egg, beaten
1/2 cup bell pepper, chopped
1/2 cup onion, chopped
3 tablespoons low calorie margarine
10 oz. rotel tomatoes, diced
1/4 teaspoon white sugar
2 tablespoons brown sugar
3 1/2 tablespoons worcestershire sauce
1 tablespoon mustard

Mix ground turkey, bread crumbs, egg, and salt. Shape into 50 small balls. Place in oblong baking dish and brown quickly. Discard fat. In saucepan, saute' bell pepper and onion in margarine until limp. Add rotel tomatoes, sugars, worcestershire sauce, and mustard. Mix well, heat and pour over meatballs. Bake at 300 degrees for 20 minutes.

Yield: 50 meatballs

Calories: 39 per two meatballs
Exchanges: 1 Meat
            1/2 Fat

Cholesterol: 5 Mg   PRO: 1 Gm
SF: less than 1 Gm   CHO: 2 Gm
Sodium: 61 Mg   Fat: 3 Gm

CRAB STUFFED MUSHROOMS

4 tablespoons green onions, chopped
1 1/2 cups crab meat
2 tablespoons diet margarine
*1 cup special white sauce
1/4 teaspoon lemon juice
Salt and pepper to taste
24 mushroom caps, large

Preheat oven to 350 degrees. Cook green onion and crab meat in margarine until warm, stirring in sauce and seasonings. Spray mushroom caps with butter flavor nonstick vegetable spray and fill. Bake on cookie sheet sprayed with Pam.

Yields: 24 mushrooms

Calories: 21 per mushroom
Exchanges: 2 mushrooms=1/2 meat

Cholesterol: 9 Mg
SF: less than 1 Gm
Sodium: 132 Mg

PRO: 2 Gm
CHO: 1 Gm
Fat: 1 Gm

*To prepare Special White Sauce, see page 139.

FLORENTINE MUSHROOMS

10 oz. package frozen chopped spinach
18 medium mushrooms
Butter flavor nonstick vegetable spray
1/2 cup defatted chicken broth
1 clove garlic, minced
1 large onion, chopped fine
1/4 cup bread crumbs
Pepper
Dry mustard
2 1/2 tablespoons grated parmesan cheese

Cook and drain chopped spinach. Wash mushrooms. Remove stems; set aside. Spray skillet with vegetable spray. Cook garlic 1 minute. Remove pan from heat. Spray mushroom caps with vegetable spray until well coated on all sides. Place on cookie sheet. Spray skillet with vegetable spray and saute' chopped mushroom stems and onions until very soft (10 minutes). Add this to spinach, crumbs, broth, and seasonings. Mix well. Fill mushroom caps with mixture. Sprinkle with parmesan cheese. Bake at 375 degrees 15 minutes.

Yield: 18

Calories: 36 per 2 mushrooms
Exchanges: 1 Vegetable

Cholesterol: less than 1 Mg   PRO: 3 Gm
SF: less than 1 Gm   CHO: 6 Gm
Sodium: 42 Mg   Fat: less than 1 Gm

STUFFED CHERRY TOMATOES

16 cherry tomatoes
Vegetable cooking spray
1/2 cup minced onion
1/2 teaspoon garlic powder
1/3 cup lite bread crumbs
3 tablespoons (3/4 oz.) finely shredded Gruyere cheese, divided
1 tablespoon Mrs. Dash
1 tablespoon rice vinegar

Cut off top of each tomato. Scoop out pulp, leaving shells intact. Invert tomato shells on paper towels; let drain. (Cut a thick slice from bottom of each tomato, if desired, to prevent it from rolling when served).

Coat a medium nonstick skillet with cooking spray and place over medium heat until hot. Add onion and garlic; saute' until tender. Combine onion mixture, bread crumbs, 2 tablespoons shredded cheese, seasonings, tomato pulp, and next 3 ingredients in a small bowl; stir well. Spoon mixture evenly into tomatoes; top with remaining 1 tablespoon cheese. Place tomatoes in oven on high until cheese melts. Serve warm. Garnish with parsley sprigs.

Yield: 16 appetizers

Calories: 28 per two tomatoes
Exchanges: 1/2 Vegetable

Cholesterol: less than 1 Mg   PRO: 1 Gm
SF: 2 Gm   CHO: 6 Gm
Sodium: 23 Mg   Fat: less than 1 Gm

BREAKFAST SHAKE

8 oz. low-fat plain yogurt
1 banana
*14 oz. unsweetened frozen strawberries
*1/2 cup unsweetened orange juice
1 cup skim milk
1 teaspoon vanilla extract
3-4 packets Equal or Sweet & Low

Mix all ingredients in blender on high until smooth.

8 oz. = 1 serving

*May substitute 14 oz. can unsweetened pineapple (add fruit and juices) for strawberries and orange juice.

Yield: 4 servings

Calories: 92
Exchanges: 1/2 Milk
                1 Fruit

Cholesterol: 1 Mg   PRO: 4 Gm
SF: 1 Gm   CHO: 19 Gm
Sodium: 75 Mg   Fat: less than 1 Gm

RUSSIAN SPICED TEA

1 1/2 cups instant Lipton tea with nutrasweet
2 large boxes diet orange gelatin
1 teaspoon cinnamon
1/4 teaspoon clove
2-3 packages Equal or Sweet & Low to taste

Put 1 teaspoon to 1 cup hot water.

Calories: 8 per cup
Exchanges: Free

SANTA'S PUNCH

2 liters (67.6 oz.) club soda
Maraschino cherries
1 (46 oz.) can pineapple juice concentrate, thawed,
    undiluted
1/2 to 1 teaspoon peppermint extract

Fill 2 ice cube trays with club soda, reserving rest of soda. Place a cherry in each ice cube section. Freeze. To serve, combine pineapple juice, orange juice, and peppermint extract. Slowly pour in remaining club soda. Add cherry-filled ice cubes.

Yield: 15 cups

Calories: 52 per cup
Exchanges: 1 Fruit

Cholesterol: 0   PRO: 0
SF: 0   CHO: 13 Gm
Sodium: 27 Mg   Fat: 0

SPICED TEA

1 can Crystal Light Lemonade
15-quart size Nestea (without Nutrasweet)
35-quart size Nestea (with Nutrasweet with lemon)
6-quart size Tang
3 regular packages Lemonade Kool-Aid (unsweetened)
3 regular size packages Orange Kool-Aid (unsweetened)
1-3 tablespoons clove
1-3 tablespoons cinnamon

Blend all ingredients.

Use one teaspoon per cup of hot water.

Calories: 8
Exchanges: 1 cup free

HOT SPICED CIDER

4 cups unsweetened apple juice
5 whole cloves
2 cinnamon sticks
6 to 7 fresh orange slices
4 packets sugar substitute
4 cinnamon sticks, if desired

In a 2-quart saucepan, combine first 4 ingredients. Bring to a boil and simmer 15 to 20 minutes. Remove from heat. Remove cloves, orange slices, and cinnamon sticks. Stir in sugar substitute. Pour into mugs. Garnish with cinnamon sticks.

Yield: 4 servings (8 oz. per serving)

Calories: 146 per serving
Exchanges: 3 Fruit

Cholesterol: 0   PRO: less than 1 Gm
SF: 0   CHO: 36 Gm
Sodium: 10 Mg   Fat: less than 1 Gm

Soups, Salads *and* Dressings

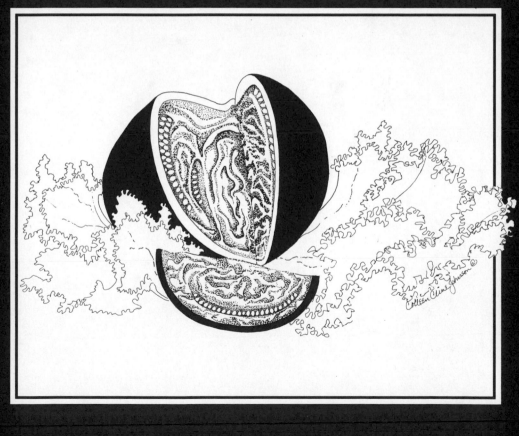

CHICKEN SOUP

4 quarts water
1 lb. chicken breasts, boneless, skinless
1 carrot, sliced
1 onion, chopped
1 rib celery, chopped
1 teaspoon salt
1 clove garlic, minced
1 teaspoon thyme
1 teaspoon basil
5 sprigs parsley
3-4 peppercorns

Cook 1 hour. Skim foam. Refrigerate chicken. Skim fat. Bring broth to a boil and add:

1 teaspoon salt
1 teaspoon pepper
3 oz. noodles
1 cup onion, chopped

3 carrots, sliced
3 ribs celery, sliced
Cubed chicken

Simmer until vegetables and noodles are tender.

Yields: 16 Cups

Calories: 70 per cup
Exchanges: 1 Meat
                      1 Vegetable

Cholesterol: 34 Mg   PRO: 8 Gm
SF: less than 1 Gm   CHO: 5 Gm
Sodium: 302 Mg   Fat: 2 Gm

COLD SPINACH SOUP

1 small onion, peeled and quartered
1 medium potato, peeled and quartered
3 cups defatted chicken broth
10 oz. fresh spinach, stems removed
1/4 teaspoon pepper
1/2 teaspoon Mrs. Dash
(Croutons and grated parmesan cheese may be used to
  garnish)

Process onion and potato in food processor until finely chopped.
Combine with chicken broth in medium saucepan and cook until
potato is tender. Process spinach until finely chopped and add to
potato mixture, cooking 5 additional minutes. Cool mixture. Return to
food processor, adding seasonings and process until smooth. Serve
hot or cold.

Yield: 4 servings

Calories: 72 per serving
Exchanges: 1/2 Bread
           1 Vegetable

Cholesterol: less than 1 Mg   PRO: 4 Gm
SF: less than 1 Gm   CHO: 14 Gm
Sodim: 352 Mg   Fat: less than 1 Gm

CREAM OF BROCCOLI SOUP

10 oz. frozen chopped broccoli
2 quarts skim milk
Pinch of white pepper
1/4 teaspoon baking soda
4 cubes chicken bouillon
4 tablespoons margarine
8 tablespoons flour

In large saucepan, combine broccoli, skim milk, white pepper, baking soda, and chicken bouillon; bring to a boil. Combine margarine and flour in a small skillet, stirring slowly with a wire whisk. When soup has reached desired thickness, return to a light boil for 5 to 8 minutes.

Yield: 8   (1 1/4-cups) servings

Calories: 169 per cup
Exchanges: 1 Milk
              1/2   Vegetable
              1 Fat

Cholesterol: 4 Mg   PRO: 11 Gm
SF: 2 Gm   CHO: 20 Gm
Sodium: 858 Mg   Fat: 5 Gm

CREAM OF TOMATO SOUP

2 cups canned crushed tomatoes
1/2 cup diced onion
1/2 teaspoon salt
1/2 bay leaf
2 tablespoons diet margarine
1 tablespoon enriched all-purpose flour
1 cup evaporated skim milk
Dash of pepper

In one-quart saucepan, combine tomatoes, onion, salt, and bay leaf; bring to a boil. Remove from heat and discard bay leaf. Transfer mixture to blender container; set aside and allow to cool slightly. In same saucepan, heat margarine over low heat until bubbly. Using a wire whisk, add flour and cook, stirring constantly, until smooth. Gradually stir in milk; continue stirring and cook until thickened. Remove from heat and set aside. Process tomato mixture in blender container until smooth. Slowly add tomato mixture to milk mixture; add pepper and stir to combine. Reheat soup over low heat before serving, stirring occasionally. (DO NOT BOIL).

Yield: 4 servings

Calories: 91 per serving
Exchanges: 1 Vegetable
1/2 Fat

Cholesterol: 3 Mg   PRO: 5 Gm
SF: less than 1 Gm   CHO: 11 Gm
Sodium: 578 Mg   Fat: 3 Gm

FOUR VEGETABLE SOUP

1 tablespoon diet margarine
1/2 cup broccoli flowerettes
1/2 cup sliced yellow squash
1 cup sliced mushrooms
1 small garlic clove, minced
1/8 teaspoon dried thyme leaves, crushed
1 (10 1/2 oz.) can condensed beef broth
1 soup can water
1 cup cooked chicken cut into strips (2-inch)
1/4 cup sliced green onions
1/4 cup red bell pepper cut into 1-inch strips

In medium size saucepan over medium heat, melt margarine. Cook mushrooms in hot margarine until browned. Add garlic, thyme, broccoli, and squash. Cook about 5 minutes until broccoli is just tender, stirring occasionally. Add soup, water, chicken, green onions, and red pepper. Cook 3 minutes longer or until heated through.

Yield: 2 servings

Calories: 215 per serving
Exchanges: 2 Meat
           2 Vegetable
           1/2 Fat

Cholesterol: 36 Mg   PRO: 19 Gm
SF: 1 Gm   CHO: 10 Gm
Sodium: 614 Mg   Fat: 11 Gm

FRESH CABBAGE SOUP

3 cups chicken broth
3 cups water
1/2 cup shredded pared carrots
1/2 cup shredded celery
1 medium potato, pared and diced
1/2 cup chopped fresh onion
2 cups chopped peeled fresh tomatoes
1 bay leaf
4 peppercorns or black pepper to taste
3 cups shredded cabbage
2 tablespoons fresh lemon juice or to taste
2 packages sugar substitute

Combine chicken broth, water, carrots, celery, potato, onion, tomatoes, bay leaf, and peppercorns in a large kettle. Simmer covered for 1 hour, stirring occasionally. Add cabbage and simmer for 10 minutes longer. Stir in lemon juice and sugar substitute. Heat.

Yield: 8 servings

Calories: 65 per serving
Exchanges: 2 Vegetable

Cholesterol: 0   PRO: 4 Gm
SF: 0   CHO: 12 Gm
Sodium: 315 Mg   Fat: less than 1 Gm

GREENS AND POTATO SOUP

1 cup frozen, thawed, chopped collard or mustard greens
1 pound round red potatoes, peeled and sliced (2 cups)
2 cups water
1 teaspoon chicken-flavored bouillon granules
Vegetable cooking spray
1 teaspoon olive oil
1 cup chopped onion
2 cloves garlic, minced
1/8 teaspoon dried whole thyme
1 (12 oz.) can evaporated skim milk
1/8 teaspoon salt
1/8 teaspoon pepper

Drain greens; squeeze out excess moisture between paper towels and set aside. Combine potatoes, water, and bouillon granules in a large dutch oven. Bring to a boil. Cover, reduce heat and simmer 15 minutes. Position knife blade in food processor bowl; add potatoes and cooking liquid. Top with cover, process until smooth. Set aside. Coat a dutch oven with cooking spray; add oil and place over medium high heat until hot. Add onion, garlic, and thyme; saute' 10 minutes, stirring occasionally. Add greens, pureed potato mixture, and remaining ingredients. Cook until thoroughly heated, stirring frequently. Serve warm.

Yield: 5 cups

Calories: 125 per cup
Exchanges: 1 Bread
1 Vegetable

Cholesterol: less than 1 Mg   PRO: 3 Gm
SF: less than 1 Gm   CHO: 26 Gm
Sodium: 93 Mg   Fat: 1 Gm

GROUND TURKEY VEGETABLE SOUP

1 1/2 pounds ground turkey
1 can (10 oz.) tomatoes
1 can (8 oz.) tomato sauce
1 cup chopped onion
1/4 cup thinly sliced fresh carrots
1 cup diced raw potatoes
1 cup chopped cabbage
1 cup diced green peppers
1 pkg. (10 oz.) frozen green beans
1 pkg. (10 oz.) frozen whole kernel corn
1 bay leaf
1/2 teaspoon basil
1/4 teaspoon pepper
1/4 teaspoon thyme
1/2 teaspoon garlic powder
6 cups water
2 tablespoons Ms. Dash

Brown meat in large skillet. Pour off fat. Add remaining ingredients. Bring mixture to a boil. Reduce heat, cover, and simmer 1 hour or until vegetables are tender. Stir occasionally. Remove bay leaf before serving.

Yield: 8 servings (2-cup servings)

Calories: 215 per serving
Exchanges: 2 1/2 Meat
           1 Bread
           1 Vegetable

Cholesterol: 54 Mg   PRO: 18 Gm
SF: 2 Gm   CHO: 20 Gm
Sodium: 205 Mg   Fat: 7 Gm

ONION SOUP GRATINE'

1 large onion, thinly sliced (1 cup)
1 tablespoon diet imitation margarine
2 (10 1/2 oz.) cans condensed beef broth
1 1/2 cups water
1/2 teaspoon worcestershire sauce
Dash pepper
6 melba toast rounds
6 tablespoons grated parmesan cheese

In large saucepan, cook onion in margarine, covered, over low heat about 20 minutes or until lightly browned, stirring occasionally. Add beef broth, water, and worcestershire sauce. Bring to boil; season with pepper. Pour into ovenproof cups or small bowls. Float melba toast on top of onion soup; sprinkle each toast piece with 1 tablespoon of the parmesan cheese. Broil 3 to 4 inches from heat about 2 minutes or until browned.

Yield: 6 servings

Calories: 63 per serving
Exchanges: 1/2 Bread
1/2 Fat

Cholesterol: 5 Mg   PRO: 2 Gm
SF: 1 Gm   CHO: 7 Gm
Sodium: 486 Mg   Fat: 3 Gm

POTATO SOUP

1 medium potato, peeled and diced
2 tablespoons chopped onion
2 tablespoons sliced celery
1/4 teaspoon instant chicken bouillon granules
1/8 teaspoon dried basil, crushed
1/4 cup frozen peas
1/2 cup skim milk
1 teaspoon corn starch

In saucepan, combine potato, onion, celery, bouillon granules, basil, 1/3 cup water, and dash pepper. Bring to boiling; reduce heat. Simmer covered 5 minutes. Add peas. Bring to boiling; reduce heat. Simmer covered about 5 minutes more. Combine milk and cornstarch; add to potato mixture. Cook and stir until bubbly. Cook and stir 2 minutes more. Place in a microwave safe container. Store in refrigerator up to 2 days. In the morning, pack in an insulated lunch box with a frozen ice pack. To serve, microwave on 100% power (high) about 3 minutes, stir once. Makes 1 serving.

Yield: 1 serving

Calories: 236
Exchanges: 2 1/2 Bread
            1/2 Vegetable
            1/2 Milk

Cholesterol: 5 Mg   PRO: 10 Gm
SF: less than 1 Gm   CHO: 49 Gm
Sodium: 116 Mg   Fat: less than 1 Gm

THREE-BEAN VEGETABLE SOUP

1 cup each dried pinto, red kidney, and small white beans, rinsed
2 medium onions, chopped
2 ribs celery, chopped
2 medium carrots, chopped
1 can chicken broth
4 cups water
1 can tomatoes, chopped
3 cloves garlic, minced
1/2 cup finely chopped parsley
1 bay leaf
Salt or salt substitute
Black pepper
Freshly grated parmesan cheese for garnish

Soak beans overnight in plenty of cold water or boil 2 minutes; cover and let stand 1 hour. Drain beans. Add 1 tablespoon of oil in dutch oven. Cook, celery and onions 3 minutes, stirring often. Add carrots, broth, water, beans, tomatoes, garlic, 1/4 cup parsley, and the bay leaf. Boil uncovered 10 minutes. Reduce heat and simmer uncovered until beans are tender, about 1 hour. Remove bay leaf. Season with salt and pepper. Stir in remaining 1/4 cup parsley. Serve soup with 1 tablespoon of freshly grated parmesan cheese.

Yield: 8 servings

Calories: 188 per serving
Exchanges: 1 Meat
             2 Bread
             1 Vegetable

Cholesterol: 4 Mg   PRO: 12 Gm
SF: 1 Gm   CHO: 35 Gm
Sodium: 397 Mg   Fat: less than 1 Gm

DUCK GUMBO

2 pounds wild duck, skinned with meat cut off bones
1 pound turkey sausage
*1/2 cup roux
3 quarts water
2 bay leaves
1 teaspoon thyme
1 tablespoon worcestershire sauce
1/4 teaspoon salt
Pepper to taste
1 tablespoon gumbo file'
1 cup chopped celery
1 cup chopped onion
1/2 cup chopped green pepper

Cook duck until done in boiling water. Brown turkey sausage in skillet until done. Drain well after cooking. Add the roux.

Add water, seasonings, and mix well. Add vegetables and simmer 1 hour. Stirring occasionally, add the drained cubed duck and sausage. Simmer 45 minutes. Serve over rice.

Yield: 12 servings

Calories: 244
Exchanges: 4 Meat
          1/2 Vegetable

Cholesterol: 60 Mg   PRO: 28 Gm
SF: 3 Gm   CHO: 6 Gm
Sodium: 241 Mg   Fat: 12 Gm

*See Page 137 for Fat Free Roux.

FISH GUMBO

1/4 teaspoon black pepper
1/4 teaspoon thyme (or use Italian seasonings)
1 lb. can tomatoes
1 (10 oz.) pkg. frozen chopped okra
2 bay leaves
1 dash tobasco
Dash cayenne
2 beef bouillon cubes
1 cup raw rice
2 tablespoons oil
1/2 teaspoon garlic, minced
1/2 cup celery
1/2 cup green peppers
1/2 cup onions
1 pound catfish

In oil, saute' 1/2 teaspoon garlic, celery, green peppers, and onions. Pour in tomatoes, okra, 2 cups of water, and cover. Simmer 30 minutes. Add fish cut up in one-inch squares. Cook 15 minutes until fish is flaky. Serve over rice.

Yield: 6 one-cup servings

Calories: 191 per cup
Exchanges: 2 1/2 Meat
              1 1/2 Vegetable
              1 Fat

Cholesterol: 3 Mg   PRO: 16 Gm
SF: 1 Gm   CHO: 16 Gm
Sodium: 320 Mg   Fat: 7 Gm

TURKEY GUMBO SOUP

Roast turkey carcass
1/2 teaspoon salt, optional
1 tablespoon margarine
1 cup sliced okra, fresh or frozen
1 cup sliced celery
1/2 cup chopped onion
1/4 cup green pepper
1 teaspoon minced garlic clove
2 tablespoons flour
1 (16 oz.) can diced tomatoes
1/2 cup rice
2 tablespoons chopped parsley
1/4 teaspoon each: cumin, pepper, tabasco sauce, thyme
8 oz. cooked turkey

Place turkey carcass in large pot and cover with water. Add salt. Simmer about 2 hours. Pour broth into container and chill. Skim off fat. Remove meat from bones and reserve. Saute' okra in margarine until it starts to turn brown, about 5 minutes. Add celery, onion, green pepper, and garlic. Saute' for about 2 minutes while stirring. Sprinkle with flour. Stir until blended and starting to brown. Add tomatoes. Add broth, rice, and seasonings. Simmer 30 minutes. Add meat and heat 5 minutes.

Yields: 8 (1 1/2 cups) servings

Calories: 115 per serving
Exchanges: 1 Meat
1 Vegetable
1/2 Bread

Cholesterol: 15 Mg   PRO: 9 Gm
SF: less than 1 Gm   CHO: 13 Gm
Sodium: 473 Mg   Fat: 3 Gm

24-HOUR SALAD

Large head of cabbage, finely shredded
1 large onion, shredded
12 packages of Sweet & Low
1/2 cup cider vinegar
1 teaspoon celery powder
1 tablespoon prepared mustard
1 cup oil free Italian dressing

Cover shredded cabbage and onion with Sweet & Low; stir well. Cover and let stand while making dressing. Bring vinegar, oil free Italian dressing, celery powder, and mustard to a boil. Cool and toss with cabbage mixture. Slaw is better the second day. Stores well in the refrigerator.

Yield: 12 (1/2 cup) servings

Calories: 36 per serving
Exchanges: 1 Vegetable

Cholesterol: 1 Mg   PRO: 2 Gm
SF: 0   CHO: 7 Gm
Sodium: 108 Mg   Fat: 0 Gm

CARROT-RAISIN-APPLE SALAD

2 medium grated carrots
*1 small grated apple
2 tablespoons raisins
1 tablespoon lite mayonnaise

Mix well. Serve on lettuce leaf.

*Drained, crushed pineapple (no sugar added) can be substituted for the apple. For a congealed salad; toss fruit mixture with sugar-free orange gelatin that has been prepared by package directions and is partially set.

Yield: 2 servings

Calories: 9 5
Exchanges: 1 Fruit
            1 Vegetable
            1 Fat

Cholesterol: less than 1 Mg   PRO: 2 Gm
SF: less than 1 Gm   CHO: 15 Gm
Sodium: 40 Mg   Fat: 3 Gm

CHICKEN RICE SALAD

2 cups cooked brown rice
2 chicken breasts (6 oz.)
1/8 teaspoon salt
1/2 cup plain low-fat yogurt
2 tablespoons lite mayonnaise
1 minced garlic clove
1 cup sliced celery
2 cups shredded raw spinach
1/4 cup chopped green onions
1 cup diced tomato
2 tablespoons lemon juice

Combine rice and chicken. Sprinkle with salt and chill. Combine yogurt, mayonnaise, and garlic. Mix with rice and chicken. Add remaining ingredients and toss lightly.

Yield: 6 servings

Calories: 146 per serving
Exchanges: 1 Meat
1 Bread
1 Vegetable

Cholesterol: 26 Mg   PRO: 12 Gm
SF: less than 1 gm   CHO: 20 Gm
Sodium: 124 Mg   Fat: 2 Gm

CHICKEN SALAD IN TOMATO

2 medium size tomatoes
2/3 cup diced cooked chicken
4 tablespoons diced celery
2 teaspoons prepared mustard
1 teaspoon chopped fresh parsley
4 teaspoons chopped green onion
1 teaspoon lite mayonnaise

With sharp knife, cut off thick slice from stem end of tomato. Scoop out seeds and pulp; coarsely chop pulp. Set aside. Combine chicken, celery, mustard, parsley, onion, mayonnaise, and reserved chopped tomato in small bowl. Lightly pack mixture into reserved tomato shell.

Yield: 2 servings

Calories: 82 per serving
Exchanges: 1 1/2 Meat
            1 Vegetable

Cholesterol: 24 Mg   PRO: 10 Gm
SF: less than 1 Gm   CHO: 6 Gm
Sodium: 239 Mg   Fat: 2 Gm

CHUNK CHICKEN AND CUCUMBER SALAD

1 can (5 oz.) chunk chicken, drained
1/2 cup chopped cucumber
2 tablespoons diagonally sliced green onion
1 tablespoon chopped, pitted ripe olives
2 tablespoons bottled lite ranch dressing
1 medium clove garlic, minced
Generous dash pepper
1 pita bread (6-inch diameter) cut in half
1 cup shredded lettuce
1/2 cup chopped tomato

In small bowl, combine all ingredients except pita bread. Toss gently
to mix. Serve in pita pocket with lettuce and tomato.

Yield: 2 servings

Calories: 239 each serving
Exchanges: 2 Meat
            1 Bread
            1/2 Vegetable
            1 Fat

Cholesterol: 38 Mg   PRO: 17 Gm
SF: 2 Gm   CHO: 18 Gm
Sodium: 695 Mg   Fat: 11 Gm

EASY COLESLAW

3 1/2 cups shredded cabbage (about 1/2 medium cabbage)
1/4 cup shredded carrots
1/4 cup chopped green pepper
2 tablespoons minced onion
1/4 cup chopped celery

DRESSING: 1/4 cup lite mayonnaise
              1 tablespoon vinegar
              1/2 teaspoon Sweet & Low
              1/2 teaspoon salt
              1/2 teaspoon celery seed

Combine all vegetables in a large bowl. Mix well and set aside. Mix together mayonnaise, vinegar, sugar, salt, and celery seed. Pour over vegetables and mix well. Refrigerate until ready to serve.

Yield: 8 servings (1/2 cup)

Calories: 46 per 1/2 cup
Exchanges: 1 Vegetable
              1/2 Fat

Cholesterol: 4 Mg   PRO: 2 Gm
SF: less than 1 Gm   CHO: 5 Gm
Sodium: 269 Mg   Fat: 2 Gm

LEMON-LIME CONGEALED SALAD

1 small package nutrasweet lime Jello
1 small package nutrasweet lemon Jello
1 small can crushed, no sugar added pineapple, drained
1/2 cup minature marshmallows
1 cup sliced bananas
2 cups diet Sprite
1/2 cup pecans, chopped

Dissolve Jello in boiling water. Add Sprite and chill. Add pineapple, marshmallows, bananas, and nuts. Pour into mold or 13 x 9-inch pan. Chill until firm.

Yield: 16 servings

Calories: 5 4
Exchanges: 1 Fruit

Cholesterol: 0	PRO: 1 Gm
SF: less than 1 Gm	CHO: 8 Gm
Sodium: 33 Mg	Fat: 2 Gm

LOW-CAL COPPER PENNIES

4 cups sliced cooked carrots, drained
1 small onion, finely chopped
1 medium bell pepper, finely chopped
1 can tomato soup
6-8 packages sugar substitute
1/2 cup oil-free Italian dressing
1/2 cup apple cider vinegar
1 tablespoon dry mustard
1 tablespoon worcestershire sauce

Combine carrots, onion, and peppers. Set aside. Bring soup, oil-free Italian dressing, vinegar, mustard, and sugar substitute to a boil. Pour hot mixture over vegetables. Refrigerate overnight. May be served hot or cold.

Yield: 16 servings

Calories: 33 per serving
Exchanges: 1 Vegetable

Cholesterol: 0   PRO: 2 Gm
SF: less than 1 Gm   CHO: 6 Gm
Sodium: 118 Mg   Fat: less than 1 Gm

MAMA BAYS' FRUIT SALAD

1 (No. 2) can chunk pineapple in own juice
2 (11 oz.) cans mandarin oranges
1 (8 oz.) can fruit cocktail own juice
1 1/2 cups low-calorie whipped topping
1/4 cup 1% low-fat cottage cheese

Drain all fruit. Toss fruit with whipped topping and cottage cheese. Refrigerate overnight.

Yield: 12 (1/2 cup) servings

Calories: 79 per serving
Exchanges: 1 Fruit
                    1 Fat

Cholesterol: 2 Mg   PRO: less than 1 Gm
SF: 2 Gm   CHO: 13 Gm
Sodium: 22 Mg   Fat: 3 Gm

MARINATED GREEN BEANS

1 pound fresh green beans
2 tablespoons peanut oil
2 tablespoons olive oil
2 tablespoons vinegar
1/4 teaspoon garlic powder
1 tablespoon prepared mustard
1/2 teaspoon crushed rosemary

Cook green beans for 10 minutes. Drain. Combine remaining ingredients and pour over beans. Marinate overnight. Serve cold.

Yield: 8 (1/2 cup) servings

Calories: 91 per serving
Exchange: 1 Vegetable
             1 Fat

Cholesterol: 0 Mg   PRO: 2 Gm
SF: 1 Gm   CHO: 5 Gm
Sodium: 26 Mg   Fat: 7 Gm

MARINATED SALAD

1 cup water
1/2 cup oil
1/4 cup sugar
1/2 cup salad vinegar (malt vinegar)
1/2 small onion, chopped
2 ribs celery, chopped
1 cup tommy toe tomatoes, halved
1 cup broccoli
1 cup carrot slices
*1 cup artichoke halves
*1 cup green beans
*1 cup baby corn, chopped
*1 cup Leseur english peas
*1 cup palm hearts, chopped

Combine water, oil, and sugar. Cook over low heat until sugar is dissolved. Add salad vinegar, pour over vegetables. Marinate 12 hours and chill before serving.

Yield: 16 servings

Calories: 80 per serving
Exchange: 1 1/2 Vegetable
          1 Fat

Cholesterol: 0   PRO: 2 Gm
SF: less than 1 Gm   CHO: 9 Gm
Sodium: 114 Mg   Fat: 4 Gm

*Use canned vegetables-double the marinade

POTATO SALAD

6 medium potatoes, cooked
1/4 cup green onion, chopped
1/4 cup celery, chopped
3 medium pimentos, chopped
3/4 cup lite mayonnaise
4 egg whites, cubed from hard boiled egg
1 teaspoon mustard
1/4 teaspoon salt (optional)
Paprika
1/4 cup sweet pickle relish

Peel and cube potatoes. Mix potatoes with green onion, celery, pimento, and cubed egg whites. Blend mayonnaise, mustard, and salt. Toss vegetables with sauce. Sprinkle with paprika.

Yield: 16 (1/2 cup) servings

Calories: 96 per serving
Exchanges: 1 Bread
             1 Fat

Cholesterol: less than 1 Mg   PRO: 2 Gm
SF: less than 1 Gm   CHO: 13 Gm
Sodium: 143 Mg   Fat: 4 Gm

STIR-FRY BEEF SALAD

1 lb. boneless beef round steak, trim fat
2 tablespoons cooking oil
1 clove garlic, minced
8 oz. fresh mushrooms, sliced (3 cups)
1 cup shredded cabbage
1 medium green pepper, cut into strips
1 medium onion, sliced and separated into rings
1 teaspoon Italian seasoning
1 teaspoon seasoned salt
1/8 teaspoon ground red pepper
1 large tomato, cut into wedges
8 oz. fresh spinach leaves

Partially freeze beef; slice thinly across the grain into bite-size strips. In wok or large skillet, cook half the beef in hot oil until browned on all sides. Remove from pan. Repeat with remaining beef and garlic; remove from pan. Add mushrooms, cabbage, green pepper strips, onion rings, Italian seasoning, seasoned salt, and red pepper to wok. Stir-fry 3 minutes or until vegetables are crisp-tender. Return beef to wok, add tomato. Cook 1 to 2 minutes or until heated through. Remove meat vegetable mixture to serving bowl. Keep warm. Add spinach leaves to wok, cover and cook for 1 minute or until slightly wilted. To serve, arrange spinach on four bowls or plates; spoon meat mixture over spinach.

Yield: 4 servings

Calories: 337 per serving
Exchanges: 4 Meat
            1 1/2 Vegetable
            1 Fat

Cholesterol: 96 Mg   PRO: 38 Gm
SF: 4 Gm   CHO: 8 Gm
Sodium: 607 Mg   Fat: 17 Gm

TARRAGON PASTA - CHICKEN SALAD

1 (8 oz.) bottle oil-free Italian dressing
2 tablespoons chopped fresh tarragon
1/2 teaspoon garlic powder
4 chicken breast halves, (1 pound), skinned and deboned
4 oz. shell macaroni, uncooked
2 cups sliced celery
1/4 cup chopped green onion
1/2 cup chopped green pepper
1/2 cup sliced carrots
1 tablespoon parsley
1/3 cup lite mayonnaise

Mix Italian dressing, garlic powder, and tarragon. Place chicken in baking dish. Pour 3/4 cup dressing mixture over chicken, reserving remaining mixture. Cover and chill 8-12 hours. Bake at 350 degrees for 25-30 minutes or until done. Drain chicken, debone, and chop.

Cook pasta according to package directions. Drain and cool. Combine chicken, remainder of dressing, pasta, and remaining ingredients in a large bowl. Toss gently. Cover and chill.

Yield: 6 servings

Calories: 232 per serving
Exchanges: 2 1/2 Meat
1 Bread
1 Vegetable
1/2 Fat

Cholesterol: 55 Mg   PRO: 22 Gm
SF: 1 Gm   CHO: 18 Gm
Sodium: 401 Mg   Fat: 8 Gm

VEGETABLE SALAD

12 oz.   chicken broth
4   medium carrots, sliced
2 cups cauliflower
2 small zucchini, diagonally sliced
1 cup sliced mushrooms
1/4 cup wine vinegar
1 package Italian dressing mix

In saucepan, bring broth to boil.   Add carrots, simmer 2-3 minutes.
Cool. Stir in remainder of ingredients. Chill 6 or more hours.

Yields: 7 cups

Calories: 65 per cup
Exchanges: 2   Vegetables

Cholesterol: 0   PRO: 4 Gm
SF: less than 1 Gm   CHO: 10 Gm
Sodium: 253 Mg   Fat: 1 Gm

WALDORF TOSS

1 small package sugar free Jello gelatin, any flavor
3/4 cup boiling water
1/2 cup cold water
Ice cubes
1 medium apple, diced
1 small banana, sliced
1/4 cup sliced celery

Dissolve gelatin in boiling water. Combine cold water and ice cubes to make 1 1/4 cups. Add to gelatin, allow to chill approximately 15 minutes. Remove any unmelted ice. Fold in fruit and celery. Chill, soft set in 30 minutes.

Yield: 5 servings

Calories: 32
Exchanges: 1 Fruit

Cholesterol: 0   PRO: 1 Gm
SF: 0   CHO: 7 Gm
Sodium: 45 Mg   Fat: 0 Gm

WARM MUSTARD GREENS SALAD

3 bunches or 6 cups fresh mustard greens
1/2 cup reduced calorie Italian dressing
Pepper, if desired

Clean mustard greens thoroughly. Remove large rib from center of each leaf. Drain in colander. Chop into smaller pieces if desired. Steam greens about 5 minutes. Toss with Italian dressing in a hot cast iron skillet just before serving. Pepper may be added.

Yield: 6 servings

Calories: 67 per serving
Exchanges: 1 Vegetable
1 Fat

Cholesterol: 0 Mg   PRO: 4 Gm
SF: less than 1 Gm   CHO: 6 Gm
Sodium: 260 Mg   Fat: 3 Gm

HOMEMADE THOUSAND ISLAND DRESSING

1 cup lite mayonnaise
1/2 cup catsup
2 teaspoons mustard
2 tablespoons pickle relish
1 egg white of boiled egg, optional

Mix all ingredients.

Yield: 1 2/3 cups

Calories: 34 per tablespoon
Exchanges: 1/2 Fat

Cholesterol: 2 Mg   PRO: 1 Gm
SF: less than 1 Gm   CHO: 3 Gm
Sodim: 107 Mg   Fat: 2 Gm

RANCH DIP

1 3/4 cups plain low-fat yogurt
1/4 cup lite mayonnaise
1 teaspoon dried parsley flakes
1 teaspoon dried minced onion
1/2 teaspoon onion powder
1/2 teaspoon garlic powder
1/2 teaspoon dill weed
1/4 teaspoon paprika
1/4 teaspoon pepper
1/4 teaspoon celery powder

Place ingredients in mixing bowl. Stir until blended and smooth. Pour into container and refrigerate 1 hour to blend flavors. Can be stored for several weeks. Use on salad greens or as dip for raw vegetables-broccoli, carrots, squash, celery, tomato, or seasonal vegetables.

Yield: 32 servings (2 cups)

Calories: 8 per serving = 1 tablespoon
Exchanges: Free

Cholesterol: 1 Mg   PRO: less than 1 Gm
SF: Less than 1 Gm   CHO: 1 Gm
Sodium: 9 Mg   Fat: less than 1 Gm

Entrees

Colleen Cline Johnson ©

BAKED CATFISH

1 pound catfish fillets
2 teaspoons powdered rosemary
1/2 teaspoon black pepper
2 fresh lemons, peeled and finely chopped
1/4 cup chopped fresh parsley
Olive oil vegetable spray

Spray pan and fish with nonstick olive oil spray. Sprinkle fish generously with powdered rosemary and black pepper. Arrange in baking dish. Bake 325 degrees 15-20 minutes or until fish flakes easily when tested with a fork. Remove to serving plate. Cover with lemons. Sprinkle with parsley.

Yield: 4 servings

Calories: 184 per   serving
Exchanges: 4 Meat

Cholesterol: 4 Mg   PRO: 20 Gm
SF: less than 1 Gm   CHO: 17 Gm
Sodium: 88 Mg   Fat: 4 Gm

BAKED FISH IN TOMATO GRAVY

1/2 cup sliced fresh mushrooms
4 green onions, chopped
1 clove garlic, minced
1/2 cup water
4 tablespoons tomato paste
1/2 teaspoon dried basil, crushed
1/2 teaspoon oregano, crushed
1/4 teaspoon sugar
1/8 teaspoon crushed red pepper
Nonstick coating spray
8 oz. fish
1/4 cup green peppers, chopped
1/2 cup shredded mozzarella cheese (2 oz.)

In a small saucepan, combine half the mushrooms, the onion, and garlic. Add water, tomato paste, basil, oregano, sugar, and red pepper. Bring to boiling; reduce heat. Simmer uncovered for 4 minutes, stirring mixture occasionally. Remove from heat.

Meanwhile, spray 2 shallow individual casseroles with the nonstick coating spray. Measure thickness of fish. Cut fish into 2 equal portions. Place fish in casserole, tucking under any thin edges.

Pour sauce over fish. Top with remaining mushrooms, green pepper, and cheese. Bake in a 450-degree oven till fish flakes easily when tested with a fork. (Allow 3 to 7 minutes per 1/2- inch thickness).

Yield: 2 servings

Calories: 265 per serving
Exchanges: 4 Meat
1 1/2 Vegetable

Cholesterol: 20 Mg   PRO: 38 Gm
SF: 3 Gm   CHO: 8 Gm
Sodium: 283 Mg   Fat: 9 Gm

BLACKENED CATFISH

1 pound catfish fillets
2 tablespoons olive oil
1 tablespoon garlic powder
1 tablespoon onion powder
1/2 teaspoon salt (optional)
1 teaspoon white pepper
1 teaspoon black pepper
1 teaspoon cayenne pepper
2 teaspoons thyme
2 teaspoons paprika
1 teaspoon oregano

Place catfish in large bowl with olive oil and let stand 30 minutes. Combine spices in a 9-inch pie plate. Heat a cast iron skillet upside down over high heat for 5-10 minutes or until very hot. Using a hot pad, turn pan right side up. Remove catfish from olive oil and drain. Dip fillets into seasoning and coat each side evenly. Put fillets into hot skillet and cook 2-3 minutes on each side, turning only once.

Yield: 4 servings

Calories: 227 per serving
Exchanges: 4 Meat
             1 Fat

Cholesterol: 4 Mg   PRO: 20 Gm
SF: 1 Gm   CHO: 12 Gm
Sodium: 307 Mg   Fat: 11 Gm

CAJUN STYLE FISH

1 1/2 cups fresh orange juice
2 tablespoons fresh lemon juice
3 tablespoons fresh lime juice
1 tablespoon rice vinegar
3 cloves garlic, peeled
2 tablespoons diced jalapeno peppers
2 tablespoons mild chili powder
2 tablespoons hot chili powder
1/2 teaspoon salt (optional)
1/4 teaspoon black pepper
1 pound perch fillets

In bowl, combine orange juice, lemon juice, lime juice, rice vinegar, garlic, jalapeno peppers, chili powders, salt, and black pepper. Let sauce stand at room temperature 3 hours.

Arrange each fillet on a sheet of aluminum foil. Bring edges of foil upward to form a bowl. Spoon 2 tablespoons of sauce over each fillet. Pinch top of edge of foil together to seal. Arrange foil packets in baking dish. Steam at 450 degrees 8-10 minutes, or until fish flakes easily when tested with a fork. Heat remaining sauce, serve with fish.

Yield: 4 servings

Calories: 204 per serving
Exchanges: 4 Meat
                      1 Fruit

Cholesterol: 4 Mg   PRO: 28 Gm
SF: less than 1 Gm   CHO: 14 Gm
Sodium: 317 Mg   Fat: 4 Gm

CATFISH CASSEROLE

*2 medium size zucchini
1 pound catfish fillets
1 medium onion, diced
1/2 cup green onions, chopped
1/2 teaspoon garlic, minced
1 large green pepper, diced
3 ribs celery, diced
4 tablespoons diet margarine
4 oz. mozzarella cheese
1 can stewed tomatoes
1/4 cup lite bread crumbs
1/4 cup parsley

Cut zucchini in 1/4-inch slices. Boil in water until medium tender (about 15-20 minutes). Saute' onion, garlic, green pepper, parsley, and celery in margarine. Place a layer of boiled zucchini in bottom of a deep casserole dish; cover with catfish. Layer with sauteed seasonings. Place tomatoes over the seasonings and sprinkle with mozzarella cheese. Cover with bread crumbs. Continue layering remaining ingredients, omitting the catfish. Bake at 350 degrees for 40 minutes.

* May substitute yellow squash.

Yield: 6 servings

Calories: 246 per serving
Exchanges: 3 Meat
                    2 Vegetable
                    1 Fat

Cholesterol: 17 Mg   PRO: 17 Gm
SF: 3 Gm   CHO: 22 Gm
Sodium: 389 Mg   Fat: 10 Gm

CATFISH ETOUFFEE

2 pounds catfish fillets, skinned and cut into 1-inch chunks
1 cup boiling water
4 tablespoons brown roux
1 cup chopped onions
1 cup chopped green onions
1/2 cup chopped celery
1/2 teaspoon garlic powder
2 cups canned tomatoes, coarsely chopped, with liquid
1 lemon slice, cut 1/4-inch thick
1 tablespoon worcestershire sauce
1 small bay leaf
1/4 teaspoon thyme
1/4 teaspoon cayenne pepper
1 teaspoon black pepper
2 teaspoons salt
1/2 cup chopped fresh parsley
4 cups cooked white rice

Add brown roux and vegetables to heavy 4-to-5 quart casserole. Set over low heat. Cook about 5 minutes or until they are soft but not brown. Stirring constantly, pour in the boiling water in a slow, thin stream. Add seasonings. Reduce the heat to low and simmer, partly covered, for 30 minutes. Add the chunks of catfish and the parsley and stir gently to moisten the fish evenly with the simmering sauce. Cover partially, without stirring, simmer for 10 minutes or until the catfish flakes easily. Serve at once with rice.
See page 137 for roux.

Yield: 8 servings

Calories: 240 per serving
Exchanges: 4 Meat
            1 Bread
            1 Vegetable

Cholesterol: 4 Mg   PRO: 25 Gm
SF: 1 Gm   CHO: 26 Gm
Sodium: 668 Mg   Fat: 4 Gm

FOIL-BAKED FISH FILLETS

Vegetable cooking spray
1 tablespoon reduced calorie margarine
2 cups fresh mushrooms, chopped
2 tablespoons minced onion
3 tablespoons chablis or other dry white wine
1 tablespoon lemon juice
2 tablespoons minced fresh parsley
1 pound fresh perch
Freshly ground black pepper

Coat a skillet with cooking spray, add margarine. Melt margarine over medium heat. Add mushrooms and onion, saute' 5 minutes or until tender. Stir in next 3 ingredients. Cook 5 minutes or until most of the liquid has evaporated.

Cut four 12-inch square pieces of heavy duty aluminum foil. Place a fillet, skin side down, in center of each piece of foil. Pepper each fillet top with 1/4 of mushroom mixture.

Fold aluminum foil over fillets and seal edges securely. Place foil packages on a baking sheet, bake at 400 degrees for 20 to 25 minutes or until fillets flake easily with a fork.

Yield: 4 servings

Calories: 173 per serving
Exchanges: 4 Meat
1 Vegetable

Cholesterol: 4 Mg   PRO: 28 Gm
SF: less than 1 Gm   CHO: 4 Gm
Sodium: 131 Mg   Fat: 5 Gm

GRILLED CATFISH

1 pound catfish fillets
1/2 cup oil free Italian dressing

Marinate fish for 30 minutes to one hour before cooking in diet Italian dressing. Prepare coals. Cover the grill with foil or use a fish basket. Grill 5-6 minutes. Turn, grill 3-5 minutes or until fish flakes easily when tested with a fork.

Yield: 4 servings

Calories: 168 per serving
Exchange: 4 Meat

Cholesterol: 4 Mg   PRO: 20 Gm
SF: less than 1 Gm   CHO: 13 Gm
Sodium: 291 Mg   Fat: 4 Gm

POACHED CATFISH

Juice of lemon
1 pound catfish fillets
1 fresh lemon quartered
Black pepper to taste

In large skillet, heat lemon juice. Add catfish fillets. Cover and poach 3-8 minutes or until fish flakes easily when tested with fork. Serve with fresh lemon and black pepper.

Yield: 4 servings

Calories: 168 per serving
Exchanges: 4 Meat

Cholesterol: 4 Mg   PRO: 20 Gm
SF: less than 1 Gm   CHO: 13 Gm
Sodium: 88 Mg   Fat: 4 Gm

SESAME OVEN FRIED FISH

1 lb. catfish fillets
1/4 cup skim milk
1/2 cup fine dry bread crumbs
1/4 cup yellow corn meal
1 tablespoon toasted sesame seed
1 tablespoon Mrs. Dash
1/4 teaspoon dry mustard
1/8 teaspoon garlic powder
Nonstick spray coating
Parsley

Thaw fish if frozen. Measure thickness of fish. Pour milk into a shallow dish. Combine crumbs, corn meal, sesame seed, mustard, garlic powder, and dash pepper. Dip fish into milk; coat with crumb mixture. Spray a 13 X 9 X 2- inch baking pan with nonstick coating. Place fish in pan. Sprinkle with parsley. Bake in 450-degree oven until golden and fish flakes easily. Allow 4-6 minutes per 2-inch thickness.

Yield: 4 servings

Calories: 216 per serving
Exchanges: 4 Meat
1 Bread

Cholesterol: 4 Mg   PRO: 22 Gm
SF: 1 Gm   CHO: 23 Gm
Sodium: 114 Mg   Fat: 4 Gm

CRAWFISH JAMBALAYA

1 large yellow onion, chopped
1 large garlic clove, minced
1 large green pepper, chopped
1 celery rib, diced with tops
1/4 cup oil
2 tablespoons minced parsley
1/2 teaspoon dried leaf thyme
2 large bay leaves
1 teaspoon tabasco pepper sauce
1 can (1lb. 2 oz.) tomatoes
1/2 cup tomato sauce
2 cups rice, uncooked
1 1/2 lbs. fresh crawfish

Saute' onion, garlic, green pepper, and celery in oil (moderate heat) until onion is golden. Add parsley, thyme, and bay leaves. Cook 5 minutes, stirring often. Add tabasco, tomatoes (and juice), tomato sauce, 2 cups water, and 2 teaspoons salt. Simmer 5 minutes.

Add rice, reduce heat to simmer and cook covered 30 minutes. Add crawfish and simmer covered 10 to 15 minutes until rice is tender and all liquid is absorbed. Season to taste with tabasco.

Yield: 8 servings

Calories: 301 per serving
Exchanges: 4 Meat
             1 Bread
             1 Vegetable
             2 Fat

Cholesterol: 134 Mg   PRO   32 Gm
SF: 2 Gm   CHO: 23 Gm
Sodium: 86 Mg   Fat: 9 Gm

GRILLED SHRIMP

1 pound large shrimp
2 tablespoons lite soy sauce
2 tablespoons Lea & Perrins
1 tablespoon molasses or honey
McCormick lite lemon pepper to taste
1/2 cup whole mushrooms
1/2 cup small whole onions
1/2 cup sliced carrots and sliced squash
1/2 sliced green and red pepper
2 cups cooked wild and regular rice

Peel and marinate shrimp at least one hour. Wash vegetables and microwave 1-2 minutes to tenderize. Alternate shrimp and vegetables on skewers. Grill and baste skewers with marinade for 2 minutes on each side. Serve with 1/2 cup cooked rice.

Yield: 4 servings

Calories: 217
Exchanges: 4 Meat
             1 Bread
             1 Vegetable

Cholesterol: 165 Mg   PRO: 32 Gm
SF: less than 1 Gm   CHO: 20 Gm
Sodium: 626 Mg   Fat: 1 Gm

SEAFOOD STUFFED EGGPLANT

1 eggplant (2 cups)
8 oz. shrimp pieces
1/2 cup chopped onion
1/4 cup chopped bell pepper
2 tablespoons dried parsley

1 garlic clove, chopped

1/4 cup chopped celery
1/8 teaspoon sugar

1/4 teaspoon white pepper
1/4 teaspoon black pepper
1/4 teaspoon salt
1/2 teaspoon thyme
2 tablespoons diet
    margarine
1 cup seasoned bread
    crumbs
10 oz. diced rotel tomatoes
2 bay leaves

Boil and scoop pulp out of eggplant. Spray skillet with olive oil cooking spray. Saute' onion, bell pepper, eggplant, parsley, and garlic. Add tomatoes, sugar, bay leaves, salt, pepper, and thyme. Simmer 5 minutes. Add shrimp and simmer an additional 3 minutes. Remove from heat, set aside. Combine margarine and bread crumbs. Alternate layers of vegetable mixture and bread crumbs to stuff eggplant. Make top layer a few spoons of bread crumbs. Bake 10 minutes at 300 degrees. Be sure to serve warm with a tossed salad.

Yield: 2 servings

Calories: 318 per serving
Exchanges: 4 Meat
             3 Vegetable
             1 Bread
             1 Fat

Cholesterol: 166 Mg   PRO: 36 Gm
SF: 1 Gm   CHO: 30 Gm
Sodium: 629 Mg   Fat: 6 Gm

SHRIMP AND CHEESE STUFFED POTATOES

6 baked potatoes, medium
Vegetable cooking spray
1/4 cup chopped onions
1 clove garlic, crushed (optional)
1/2 teaspoon parsley
1 (6 oz.) pkg. baby shrimp, deveined and cooked
1/4 cup diet margarine
1/2 cup warm skim milk
1/2 teaspoon salt or substitute
1/4 teaspoon pepper
1/2 cup shredded low-fat cheddar cheese
Paprika

Cut a thick slice from the top of each potato. Scoop out the pulp, reserve the shell and pulp for later use. Saute' the onions, garlic, parsley, and shrimp, just a minute or two, in vegetable cooking spray. Mix margarine, milk, salt, pepper, and cheese with potato pulp until thoroughly combined and the texture is relatively smooth. Combine mixture that has been sauteed with the potato mixture. Stuff potatoes and garnish by sprinkling paprika on top of each. Broil stuffed potatoes just until warm before serving.

Yield: 6 servings

Calories: 223 per potato
Exchanges: 1 Meat
                   2 Bread
                   1 Fat

Cholesterol: 86 Mg   PRO   14 Gm
SF: 3 Gm   CHO: 35 Gm
Sodium: 411 Mg   Fat: 3 Gm

SHRIMP CREOLE

1 (16 oz.) can tomatoes

1/2 cup chopped onion
1/2 cup chopped celery
1 clove garlic, minced
3 tablespoons oil
1 (8 oz.) can tomato sauce
1 teaspoon salt

1/2 to 1 teaspoon chili powder
1 tablespoon worcestershire
Dash hot pepper sauce
2 teaspoons corn starch
1 lb. cleaned raw shrimp
1/2 cup green peppers

Cook onion, celery, and garlic in hot oil until tender, but not brown. Add tomatoes and tomato sauce, salt, chili, worcestershire, and pepper sauce. Simmer uncovered 20 minutes. Mix corn starch with 1 tablespoon cold water; stir into sauce. Cook and stir until mixture thickens and bubbles. Add shrimp and green pepper. Cover. Simmer until done, about 5 mintues. Serve over rice.

Yield: 6 servings

Calories: 131 per serving
Exchanges: 2 1/2 Meat
1 Vegetable
1 Fat

Cholesterol: 110 Mg
SF: less than 1 Gm
Sodium: 664 Mg

PRO: 17 Gm
CHO: 9 Gm
Fat: 3 Gm

SHRIMP SAUTE'

1 pound fresh shrimp
3 tablespoons diet margarine, melted
1 cup sliced fresh mushrooms
1 small onion, sliced and separated into rings
1/4 cup dry white wine
1 diced tomato
1 teaspoon garlic powder
1 teaspoon seafood seasoning *(Decrease seafood seasoning too spicy c̄ 1 tsp)*
1 teaspoon parsley

Saute' shrimp in margarine in large skillet until they appear pink. Drain and set aside, reserving drippings in skillet.

Saute' mushrooms and onion in drippings in skillet 4 minutes or until tender. Drain and set aside, reserving drippings in skillet.

Add wine, shrimp, and seafood seasoning blend to drippings in skillet. Cook over high heat until mixture is reduced by about half. Add shrimp, mushrooms, onions, and tomato to drippings in skillet. Cook over high heat 1 minute or until heated. Serve immediately.

Yield: 4 servings

Calories: 197 per serving
Exchanges: 4 Meat
            1 Vegetable
            1 Fat

Cholesterol: 168 Mg   PRO: 30 Gm
SF: 1 Gm   CHO: 8 Gm
Sodium: 178 Mg   Fat: 5 Gm

SHRIMP SCAMPI

1 1/4 lbs. shelled and deveined medium shrimp
4 tablespoons lemon juice
1 1/2 tablespoons diet margarine, melted
2 large or 4 small garlic cloves, crushed
*1/2 teaspoon each salt, pepper, paprika
Parsley sprigs for garnish

Preheat broiler. In a shallow 2-quart flameproof casserole, arrange shrimp. In small bowl, combine remaining ingredients except parsley; pour mixture over shrimp and toss to coat. Broil 3-4 inches from heat source until shrimp are golden brown, 1-2 minutes. Garnish with parsley.

Yield: 4 servings

Calories: 178 per serving
Exchanges: 5 Meat

Cholesterol: 210 Mg   PRO: 35 Gm
SF: less than 1 Gm   CHO: 5 Gm
Sodium: 613 Mg   Fat: 2 Gm

* May omit salt or use salt substitute.

SHRIMP-CHICKEN JAMBALAYA

Vegetable cooking spray
2 medium onions, chopped
2 cloves garlic, minced
2 ribs celery, chopped
1 large green pepper, chopped
2/3 cup uncooked regular rice
2 cups chicken broth
8 oz. chicken breast, cooked and cubed
1 (16 oz.) can stewed tomatoes
8 oz. shrimp deveined and rinsed
1/2 teaspoon hot sauce
1/4 teaspoon pepper

Coat a large skillet with cooking spray; place over medium heat until hot. Add onion, garlic, celery, and green pepper; saute' until tender. Add remaining ingredients. Bring to a boil, cover, reduce heat, and simmer 25 minutes or until rice is done, stirring occasionally.

Yields: 4 servings.

Calories: 311 per serving
Exchanges: 4 Meat
             1 Bread
             3 Vegetable

Cholesterol: 129 Mg   PRO: 36 Gm
SF: 1 Gm   CHO: 35 Gm
Sodium: 650 Mg   Fat: 3 Gm

BAKED CHICKEN WITH VEGETABLES

6 (4 oz.) chicken breasts, cut up and skinned
3 medium carrots
2 ribs celery
3 medium potatoes
1 (15 oz.) can tomato sauce with tomato pieces
1 tablespoon oregano
Garlic powder if desired
Pepper to taste
2 teaspoons dried parsley
Nonstick vegetable spray

Cut vegetables into pieces. Spray a 9 X 13-inch pan with nonstick vegetable spray. Arrange vegetables on bottom and chicken on top. Sprinkle lightly with garlic powder, if desired.

Pour tomato sauce over all. Sprinkle with oregano, pepper, and dried parsley.

Cover with foil and bake in oven for 1 1/2 hours at 350 degrees. This recipe is excellent prepared in a crockpot.

Yield: 6 servings

Calories: 244 per serving
Exchanges: 4 Meat
             1 Bread
             1 Vegetable

Cholesterol: 73 Mg   PRO: 30 Gm
SF: less than 1 Gm   CHO: 22 Gm
Sodium: 118 Mg   Fat: 4 Gm

CAJUN-SPICED CHICKEN

1 cup vegetable juice cocktail
2 tablespoons red wine vinegar
1-2 teaspoons hot sauce
1/2 teaspoon dried whole oregano
1/2 teaspoon garlic powder
4 (4 oz. each) chicken breasts, skinned
2 tablespoons chopped celery
2 tablespoons diced green bell pepper
2 tablespoons chopped onion
1 tablespoon corn starch
4 cups hot, cooked regular rice (without salt or fat)

Combine first 5 ingredients in shallow container. Add chicken and marinate in refrigerator 30 minutes. Remove chicken from marinade, reserving marinade. Place chicken on a microwave-safe glass platter; cover with heavy-duty plastic wrap, turning back 1 corner to vent. Microwave at high 8-10 minutes or until chicken is done, giving dish a quarter turn at 2-minute intervals. Let chicken stand, covered, 5 minutes.

Combine celery, bell pepper, and onion in a 1-quart glass measure; microwave at high 3 to 4 minutes or until vegetables are tender, stirring once. Combine reserved marinade and corn starch, stirring until smooth. Add to vegetable mixture and microwave uncovered at high 1 to 2 minutes or until thickened.

Yield: 8 servings

Calories: 182 per serving
Exchanges: 2 Meat
            1 Bread

Cholesterol: 48 Mg   PRO: 19 Gm
SF: less than 1 Gm   CHO: 22 Gm
Sodium: 60 Mg   Fat: 2 Gm

CHEESY STUFFED POTATO

1 medium baking potato
1 (6 1/2 oz.) can water-packed chicken, drained and flaked
1 tablespoon minced onion
1 tablespoon finely chopped celery
1 tablespoon finely chopped green pepper
3 tablespoons reduced calorie mayonnaise
1/4 teaspoon seasoned pepper
Paprika
2 tablespoons shredded low-fat cheddar cheese

Wash potato, bake at 375 degrees for 45 to 60 minutes or until done. Let stand until cool enough to handle. Cut potato in half lengthwise; scoop out pulp, leaving a 1/4-inch thick shell.

Mash potato pulp in a medium bowl with a potato masher or fork; stir in next 6 ingredients, mixing well. Divide mixture evenly into potato shells. Sprinkle each with paprika. Place on a baking sheet, bake at 350 degrees for 10 minutes. Remove from oven and sprinkle with cheese. Bake an additional 5 minutes or until thoroughly heated.

Yield: 2 servings

Calories: 233 per serving
Exchanges: 3 Meat
                   1 Bread
                   2 Fat

Cholesterol: 82 Mg   PRO: 23 Gm
SF: 2 Gm   CHO: 15 Gm
Sodium: 460 Mg   Fat: 9 Gm

CHICKEN AND DUMPLINGS

1/2 lb. skinned, boned chicken
3 ribs celery
1/2 teaspoon salt
Pepper to taste
1 cup peas
1 cup sliced carrots

4 cups flour
1 stick margarine
4 teaspoons baking powder
1 teaspoon salt
1 1/2 cups boiling water
2 quarts water

Throw all ingredients into a large pot. Bring to a boil and cook until chicken is tender. Cool in the refrigerator at least 6-8 hours. Skim all fat from the top of chilled broth.

Add enough water to chicken and broth to make 2 quarts. Bring to a boil. Add dumplings. Cover and simmer 12-15 minutes. Set aside 10 minutes.

To prepare dumplings, mix flour, baking powder, and salt. Blend in margarine. Pour in boiling water. Roll out on a floured board and cut into strips. May substitute 4 cups self-rising flour for flour, baking powder, and salt.

Yield: 12   servings

Calories: 248 per serving
Exchanges: 1 Meat
             2 Bread
             2 Fat

Cholesterol: 12 Mg   PRO: 10 Gm
SF: 2 Gm   CHO: 34 Gm
Sodium: 351 Mg   Fat: 8 Gm

CHICKEN BREASTS WITH ROSEMARY

4 (4 oz. each) chicken breasts, skinless, boneless
Powdered rosemary
Black pepper
1 large yellow onion, quartered
Garlic powder

Rub skinned and boned chicken with rosemary, black pepper, and garlic powder. Place onion on top of chicken. Place breasts of chicken in oven, covered, at 375 degrees for 45-60 minutes.

Yield: 4 servings

Calories: 152 per serving
Exchanges: 4 Meat

Cholesterol: 72 Mg   PRO: 28 Gm
SF: 1 Gm   CHO: 1 Gm
Sodium: 95 Mg   Fat: 4 Gm

CHICKEN BROCCOLI SKILLET

1 (10 oz.) package frozen cut broccoli
4 (4 oz.) chicken breasts, boneless, skinless
1/4 cup chopped onion
Butter flavored nonstick vegetable spray
1 teaspoon lemon juice
1/2 teaspoon McCormick lite poultry seasoning
3 medium tomatoes, cut in wedges
Pepper

Thaw broccoli. Cook chicken and onion quickly in vegetable spray until just done. Stir broccoli, lemon juice, lite poultry seasoning, and 1/8 teaspoon pepper. Cook, uncovered, 6 minutes. Add tomatoes, cook covered 3 to 4 minutes.

Yield: 4 servings

Calories: 200 per serving
Exchanges: 4 Meat
                2 Vegetable

Cholesterol: 72 Mg   PRO: 32 Gm
SF: 1 Gm   CHO: 9 Gm
Sodium: 119 Mg   Fat: 4 Gm

CHICKEN CACCIATORE

4 (4 oz.) boneless, skinless chicken breasts
2 cups fresh mushrooms, sliced
1 green pepper, finely diced
2 onions, thinly sliced
1 clove garlic, minced
Butter flavored cooking spray
2 cups chopped tomatoes
1/4 teaspoon basil
1/2 teaspoon dried oregano
1/2 teaspoon pepper
1/2 cup water or dry red wine

In a heavy saucepan, saute' mushrooms, green pepper, onions, and garlic in vegetable cooking spray. Add chicken breasts and brown lightly. Add tomatoes, basil, oregano, pepper, and wine or water. Cover and cook over low heat 1 1/2 hours or until chicken is tender.

Yield: 4 servings

Calories: 212 per serving
Exchanges: 4 Meat
           2 Vegetable

Cholesterol: 72 Mg   PRO: 33 Gm
SF: 1 Gm   CHO: 11 Gm
Sodium: 103 Mg   Fat: 4 Gm

CHICKEN CATALINA

4 (4 oz.) chicken breasts, skinned
1/4 teaspoon pepper
1/2 cup diet catalina dressing

Marinate chicken breasts in dressing overnight. Prepare coals. Grill chicken 20 minutes over hot grill, brushing with remainder of catalina dressing.

Yield: 4 servings

Calories: 176 per serving
Exchanges: 4 Meat
             1/2 Fruit

Cholesterol: 72 Mg   PRO: 28 Gm
SF: 1 Gm   CHO: 7 Gm
Sodium: 339 Mg   Fat: 4 Gm

CHICKEN CONTINENTAL

4 (4 oz.) chicken breasts, cooked and cubed
1 can mushrooms (4 oz.), sliced and drained or
1 cup fresh mushrooms
1 clove garlic, crushed
1 can chicken broth
1 package (10 oz.) chopped broccoli
1/2 teaspoon basil leaves
1 1 /2 cups dry Minute rice
Dash pepper
Nonstick vegetable cooking spray

Saute' chicken, mushrooms, and garlic in cooking spray 2-3 minutes. Add remaining ingredients except rice and bring to a boil. Stir in rice, remove from heat, cover and let stand 5 minutes.

Yield: 4 servings

Calories: 251 per serving
Exchanges: 4 Meat
           1 Vegetable
           1 Bread

Cholesterol: 72 Mg   PRO: 35 Gm
SF: 1 Gm   CHO: 21 Gm
Sodium: 318 Mg   Fat: 4 Gm

CHICKEN NAPOLI

4 (4 oz.) large chicken breasts
2 cans french onion soup
2 cans stewed tomatoes
Mrs. Dash seasoning

Cook chicken until tender. Remove from bones and cut into bite size pieces. Combine soup, tomatoes, chicken, and Mrs. Dash seasoning in a deep skillet. Heat to just under boiling and reduce to simmer for 30 minutes. Thicken with corn starch or flour if desired. Serve over rice.*

*May serve over pasta.

Yield: 4 servings

Calories: 201 per serving
Exchanges: 4 Meat
             1 1/2 Vegetable

Cholesterol: 72 Mg   PRO: 31 Gm
SF: 1 Gm   CHO: 8 Gm
Sodium: 541 MG   Fat: 5 Gm

CHICKEN POT PIE

1/2 cup liquid butter substitute (1 pkg. Butter Buds mixed
   with 1/2 cup water)
3 tablespoons flour
1/4 cup onion, chopped
1/4 cup celery, sliced
16 oz. frozen mixed vegetables
3 cups defatted chicken broth
1 cup skim milk
3 cups diced chicken breasts
9-inch pie crust, uncooked

Combine butter substitute and flour in saucepan over low heat.
Gradually add chicken broth and milk, stirring constantly until
smooth and thickened. Saute' celery and onion in vegetable spray.
Stir in chicken, salt, pepper, mixed vegetables, onion, and celery.
(Cook vegetables by package instructions). Mix well. Pour into a 13
x 9 x 2-inch baking dish. Roll pastry to 1/8-inch thickness on lightly
floured board and cut into 11-inch wide strips. Arrange in lattice
design over chicken mixture. Bake at 350 degrees for 30 minutes or
until pastry is golden brown.

Yield: 9 servings

Calories: 211
Exchanges: 2 Meat
           1 Bread
           1/2 Vegetable

Cholesterol: 36 Mg   PRO: 18 gm
SF: 1 Gm   CHO: 28 Gm
Sodium: 515 Mg   Fat: 3 Gm

USE: Mama Bays' pie crust, page 211 .

CHICKEN-VEGETABLE TETRAZZINI

4 (4 oz.) skinned chicken breast halves, cut into 1/2 strips
2 cloves garlic, minced
1 cup frozen peas and carrots
1 cup fresh mushrooms, quartered
1 tablespoon diet margarine
2 tablespoons all-purpose flour
3/4 cup plus 2 tablespoons skim milk
2 tablespoons diced pimento
1/4 teaspoon salt (optional)
1/4 teaspoon pepper
2 cups hot cooked spaghetti (cooked without salt or fat)

Place chicken and garlic in a 2-quart glass measure. Cover with heavy-duty plastic wrap and vent. Microwave at medium-high (70% power) 4 minutes, stirring once. Add peas and carrots. Cover and microwave at medium-high 4 minutes, stirring once. Stir in mushrooms; cover and microwave medium-high 2 to 3 minutes or just until chicken is done. Drain well and set aside. Place margarine in a 2-cup glass measure. Microwave until margarine melts. Add flour, stir well. Gradually add milk, stirring well. Microwave at high 4 minutes or until thickened and bubbly, stirring twice. Stir in pimento and next 2 ingredients; set aside. Combine chicken mixture and pasta in a large bowl. Spoon sauce over chicken mixture, toss well.

Yield: 4 servings (1 1/2 cups)

Calories: 292 per serving
Exchanges: 4 Meat
            2 Bread

Cholesterol: 74 Mg   PRO: 34 Gm
SF: 2 Gm   CHO: 30 Gm
Sodium: 297 Mg   Fat: 4 Gm

CRUNCHY SPICED CHICKEN

2 cups herb-seasoned stuffing mix, finely crushed
1 1/2 teaspoons garlic powder
1 1/2 teaspoons pepper
3/4 teaspoon paprika
1/4 to 1/2 teaspoon poultry seasoning
1/2 cup skim milk
1/4 cup egg substitute
4 (4 oz.) chicken breasts, skinned

Combine first 5 ingredients in a plastic bag. Shake to mix and set aside. Combine milk and egg. Mix well and set aside.

Place 2 or 3 pieces of chicken in bag. Shake well, dip chicken in egg mixture, return to bag, and shake again. Repeat procedure with remaining chicken. Press coating into place, if necessary. Place chicken, bone side down, on a microwave roasting rack, arranging meatier pieces to the outside. Cover with waxed paper. Microwave chicken at high for 10 minutes.

Rearrange chicken so lesser-cooked pieces are to the outside. Microwave at high 8 to 11 minutes or until juices run clear and meat near bone is no longer pink.

Yield: 4 servings

Calories: 363 per serving
Exchanges: 4 Meat
1 Bread
2 Fat

Cholesterol: 72 Mg   PRO: 31 Gm
SF: 4 Gm   CHO: 26 Gm
Sodium: 335 Mg   Fat: 15 Gm

HERBED CHICKEN PICCATA

6 (4 oz.) chicken breast halves, skinned and boned
1/3 cup all-purpose flour
1 1/2 teaspoons poultry seasoning blend
1/4 cup plus 2 tablespoons diet margarine
1/4 cup lemon juice
1 lemon, thinly sliced

Place each piece of chicken between 2 sheets of wax paper and flatten to 1/4-inch thickness with meat mallet or rolling pin. Combine flour and poultry seasoning blend. Dredge chicken in flour mixture.

Melt 1/4 cup margarine in large skillet over medium heat. Add chicken and cook 3 to 4 minutes on each side until golden brown. Remove chicken and drain on paper towels. Place on serving platter; keep warm. Add lemon juice and lemon slices to pan drippings in skillet; cook until thoroughly heated. Pour lemon mixture over chicken.

Yield: 6 servings

Calories: 225 per serving
Exchanges: 4 Meat
             1 Fat

Cholesterol: 72 Mg   PRO: 29 Gm
SF: 1 Gm   CHO: 7 Gm
Sodium: 152 Mg   Fat: 9 Gm

LEMON CHICKEN

1 lb. skinned, boned chicken breasts, cut into strips
1 medium onion, chopped
1/2 teaspoon garlic powder
2 tablespoons diet margarine
1 tablespoon corn starch
1 can (13 3/4 oz.) chicken broth
1 large carrot, sliced diagonally
2 tablespoons fresh lemon juice
*1/2 teaspoon salt
1 cup french cut green beans
3 tablespoons chopped parsley
1 1/2 cups dry Minute rice

Saute' chicken, onion, and garlic in margarine until lightly browned, about 5 minutes. Stir in corn starch and cook 1 minute.

Add broth, carrot, lemon juice, and salt. Bring to a full boil. Stir in green beans, parsley, and rice. Cover; remove from heat. Let stand 5 minutes. Fluff with a fork.

Yield: 4 servings

Calories: 291 per serving
Exchanges: 4 Meat
          1 Bread
          1 Vegetable

Cholesterol: 72 Mg   PRO: 39 Gm
SF: 2 Gm   CHO: 18 Gm
Sodium: 740 Mg   Fat: 7 Gm

* Salt may be omitted to lower sodium content.

MOCK CORDON BLEU

4 (4 oz.) chicken breasts, boneless, skinless
2 oz. very thinly sliced turkey ham
1 oz. (1 slice) part-skim milk mozzarella cheese
1 small tomato, chopped
1/4 cup Italian seasoned bread crumbs
1 tablespoon grated parmesan cheese
1 tablespoon snipped parsley
1 tablespoon diet margarine

Place chicken pieces between 2 pieces of plastic wrap. Pound to 1/4-inch thickness. Place 1/4 of the ham and cheese on each chicken piece. Top with 1/4 of the tomato. Roll up jelly-roll style, tucking in sides to seal well. Stir together bread crumbs, parmesan, parsley, and 1/8 teaspoon pepper. Brush chicken rolls with melted margarine. Roll in crumb mixture to coat well. Place in 10 x 6 x 2-inch baking dish. Bake at 350 degrees about 25 minutes or until chicken is done.

Yield: 4 servings

Calories: 328 per serving
Exchanges: 4 Meat
             1 Fat

Cholesterol: 117 Mg   PRO: 34 Gm
SF: 3 Gm   CHO: 30 Gm
Sodium: 367 Mg   Fat: 8 Gm

MUFFIN DIVAN

12 oz. chicken breasts, cooked, chopped
1 cup mushroom slices
1/3 cup picante sauce
2 tablespoons lite mayonnaise
2 tablespoons green onions, sliced
3 English muffins, split and toasted
1 cup chopped cooked broccoli
6 slices liteline cheese

Combine chicken, mushrooms, picante sauce, lite mayonnaise, and onions. Mix lightly. Top muffin halves with chicken mixture and broccoli. Place on ungreased cookie sheet. Bake at 350 degrees for 10 minutes. Top with liteline cheese and continue baking until cheese begins to melt.

Yield: 6 sandwiches

Calories: 201 per sandwich
Exchange: 3 Meat
             1 Bread
             1/2 Vegetable

Cholesterol: 60 Mg   PRO: 21 Gm
SF: 5 Gm   CHO: 18 Gm
Sodium: 716 Mg   Fat: 5 Gm

OVEN FRIED CHICKEN

6   (4 oz.) skinless, boneless chicken breasts
18 saltine cracker squares, crushed
2 tablespoons grated parmesan cheese
3/4 teaspoon pepper
1/2 teaspoon each: Basil, celery seed, onion powder, oregano, paprika
3/8 teaspoon salt
1/4 cup evaporated skim milk
1 tablespoon vegetable oil

Combine cracker crumbs, cheese, pepper, basil, celery seed, onion powder, oregano, paprika, and salt in bowl.   Dip chicken in evaporated milk and then coat with crumb mixture.   Place in lightly greased shallow roasting pan.   Bake in 400-degree oven for 30 minutes.   Brush with oil and bake 10 minutes longer.

Yield: 6 servings

Calories: 210 per serving
Exchanges: 4 Meat
             1/2 Bread
             1/2 Fat

Cholesterol: 72 Mg   PRO: 30 Gm
SF: 2 Gm   CHO: 9 Gm
Sodium: 469 Mg   Fat: 6 Gm

PAN FRIED CHICKEN

4 (4 oz. each) whole chicken breasts, skinned, boned, and halved

Preheat a nonstick skillet over medium heat. Add chicken breasts and brown 10 minutes on each side. Reduce heat. Cook 15-20 minutes, turning occasionally.

Variations: Rub with lite lemon pepper or Mrs. Dash.

Yield: 4 servings

Calories: 148 per serving
Exchanges: 4 Meat

Cholesterol: 72 Mg   PRO: 28 Gm
SF: 1 Gm   CHO: 0 Gm
Sodium: 63 Mg   Fat: 4 Gm

PARMESAN CHICKEN BAKE

1/2 cup dry bread crumbs
2 tablespoons grated parmesan cheese
1 tablespoon parsley flakes
1 teaspoon salt
1/8 teaspoon lemon pepper
1/8 teaspoon thyme
6 (4 oz.) chicken breasts, skinned
3 tablespoons melted margarine

Preheat oven to 350 degrees. Combine bread crumbs, cheese, and seasonings in shallow dish. Dip chicken in crumb mixture. Coat both sides. Melt margarine in baking dish in oven. Add chicken, turning to coat both sides with margarine. Bake uncovered for one hour.

Yield: 3 servings

Calories: 221 per serving
Exchanges: 4 Meat
1 Fat

Cholesterol: 75 Mg   PRO: 30 Gm
SF: 1 Gm   CHO: 5 Gm
Sodium: 523 Mg   Fat: 9 Gm

POACHED CHICKEN

4 cups chicken stock, defatted
4 (4 oz.) chicken breasts, skinned, boned, and halved
1/4 cup celery, chopped
1/4 onion, chopped

Bring stock to a boil, add chicken, and bring to a second boil. Cook 20
minutes on reduced heat until done.

Variations: Substitute turkey breasts for chicken breasts.

Yield: 4 servings

Calories: 152 per serving
Exchanges: 4 Meat

Cholesterol: 72 Mg   PRO: 28 Gm
SF: 1 Gm   CHO: 1 Gm
Sodium: 65 Mg   Fat: 4 Gm

QUICK CHICKEN STROGANOFF

4 (4 oz.) chicken breasts, boneless, skinned
1/4 teaspoon salt
1 cup sliced mushrooms
1 tablespoon chopped green onions
1/4 cup chicken broth
1/2 teaspoon thyme
1/8 teaspoon paprika
1 teaspoon corn starch
2 tablespoons water
1/4 cup white wine
1/4 cup low-fat imitation sour cream
Vegetable cooking spray
1 teaspoon diet margarine

Cut each chicken breast into strips. Spray skillet with vegetable cooking spray. Sprinkle chicken with salt and add to skillet, turning often to brown on all sides. Add mushrooms, onion, diet margarine, chicken broth, thyme, and paprika. Mix corn starch with water. Add to skillet. Simmer 2 to 3 minutes, stirring constantly until sauce thickens. Stir in wine. Cook covered on low heat 4 minutes. Stir in sour cream, mixing thoroughly. Do not boil. Serve over rice, noodles, or toast cups.

Yield: 4 servings

Calories: 178 per serving
Exchanges: 4 Meat
           1 Fat

Cholesterol: 73 Mg   PRO: 28 Gm
SF: 2 Gm   CHO: 3 Gm
Sodium: 323 Mg   Fat: 6 Gm

SKILLET CHICKEN AND RICE

1 pound boneless chicken breasts
Vegetable cooking spray
3 cups sliced fresh mushrooms
4 medium carrots, peeled and bias sliced 1/2-inch thick
3/4 cup long grain rice
1/2 cup chopped onion
1 teaspoon poultry seasoning
1 teaspoon instant chicken bouillon granules

Spray a 12-inch skillet with vegetable cooking spray. Brown chicken pieces on all sides over medium heat about 15 minutes. Remove chicken. Drain fat from skillet, if necessary. Add mushrooms, carrots, rice, onion, bouillon, poultry seasoning, 2 cups water, and 1/4 teaspoon salt. Place chicken atop rice mixture. Cover, simmer 30 minutes or until chicken and rice are done.

Yield: 6 servings

Calories: 200 per serving
Exchanges: 3 Meat
            1 Bread
            1 Vegetable

Cholesterol: 54 Mg   PRO: 18 Gm
SF: 1 Gm   CHO: 23 Gm
Sodium: 63 Mg   Fat: 4 Gm

SPINACH-STUFFED CHICKEN ROLLS

1 small onion, chopped
1/4 lb. fresh mushrooms, sliced
1 (10 oz.) package frozen chopped spinach, drained
1/4 cup grated parmesan cheese
1/2 teaspoon dried basil
1/4 teaspon salt
1/4 teaspoon hot sauce
8 (4 oz.) chicken breasts halved, skinned and boned
1 (16 oz.) can whole tomatoes, drained and chopped
1 clove garlic, crushed
1/4 teaspoon freshly ground pepper
2 to 3 teaspoons tomato paste

Combine onion and mushrooms in a 1 1/2-quart casserole. Cover and microwave at high for 4 to 4 1/2 minutes or until onion is tender; drain. Add spinach, parmesan cheese, and seasonings to onion mixture. Mix well. Place chicken breasts between 2 sheets of waxed paper, flatten to 1/4-inch thickness using a meat mallet. Place 1/4 cup spinach mixture in center of each piece. Roll up and secure with wooden pick. Place roll, seam side down, in a shallow 2-quart casserole dish.

Combine next 4 ingredients. Pour evenly over chicken rolls. Cover with waxed paper and microwave at high for 12 to 14 minutes or until done. Rotate dish after 5 minutes, and rearrange rolls so uncooked portions are to outside of dish.

Yield: 8 servings

Calories: 198 per serving
Exchanges: 4 Meat
             1 Vegetable

Cholesterol: 96 Mg   PRO: 30 Gm
SF: 1 Gm   CHO: 6 Gm
Sodium: 315 Mg   Fat: 6 Gm

STIR-FRY CHICKEN AND VEGETABLES

4 oz. chicken breast (cut into thin slices)
1 cup celery, chopped
1 cup sliced carrots
1 cup broccoli flowerettes
1 cup chicken broth (defatted)
1/4 teaspoon sugar substitute
1 tablespoon peanut oil
1 cup yellow squash, sliced
1 cup mushroom, sliced
1 clove garlic (crushed)
2 teaspoons lite soy sauce
1/2 teaspoon ginger powder
Pepper to taste
1 teaspoon corn starch

Put wok on high heat, pour in peanut oil and heat until oil sizzles. Stir in garlic. Add the chicken, stir-fry for 2 to 3 minutes until golden brown. Combine the soy sauce and ginger powder. Mix well and add to the meat in the wok, then stir-fry for 1 minute and add the celery, mushrooms, broccoli, squash and carrots. Stir-fry for 3 more minutes. Add beef stock, place the cover on the wok and allow to cook for 2 minutes. Remove the cover, add the corn starch, pepper, and sugar and stir-fry until the gravy is thick and smooth. Serve over boiled rice.

Yield: 2 servings

Calories: 277 per serving
Exchanges: 2 Meat
                     4 Vegetable
                     1 Fat

Cholesterol: 48 Mg   PRO: 26 Gm
SF: 2 Gm   CHO: 23 Gm
Sodium: 605 Mg   Fat: 9 Gm

THREE-CHEESE CHICKEN BAKE

8 oz. lasagna noodles
1/2 cup chopped onion
1/2 cup chopped green pepper
1 (10 3/4 oz.) can condensed cream of chicken soup
1 (4 oz.) can sliced mushrooms, drained
1/2 cup chopped pimento
1/3 cup skim milk
1/2 teaspoon dried basil
1 1/2 cups low-fat cottage cheese
8 oz. chopped cooked chicken or turkey
6 oz. liteline American cheese
1/2 cup grated parmesan cheese

Cook lasagna noodles in boiling water according to package directions; drain well. In saucepan, cook onion and green pepper in small amount of water until tender; drain, add soup, mushrooms, pimento, milk, and basil to vegetables in saucepan. Lay half the noodles in a 13 x 9 x 2-inch baking pan. Top with half each of the soup mixture, cottage cheese, chopped chicken, American cheese, and parmesan cheese. Repeat layers of noodles, soup mixture, cottage cheese, and chicken. Bake covered in a 350-degree oven for 45 minutes. Top with remaining American and parmesan cheese. Bake uncovered 2 minutes more or until cheese is melted.

Yield: 9 servings

Calories: 195 per serving
Exchanges: 2 Meat
             1 Bread
             1 Fat

Cholesterol: 54 Mg   PRO: 17 Gm
SF: 5 Gm   CHO: 16 Gm
Sodium: 609 Mg   Fat: 7 Gm

WINE AND CITRUS CHICKEN

4 (4 oz.) chicken breasts, skinned
1/4 teaspoon salt
1/4 teaspoon pepper
1/4 teaspoon onion powder
1/4 teaspoon paprika
1 tablespoon diet margarine
1 cup orange juice
1 cup white table wine
1 teaspoon worcestershire sauce
1/4 teaspoon garlic powder
2 tablespoons corn starch
1/4 cup water
3 packets sugar substitute

Lightly sprinkle chicken pieces with first 4 ingredients. Place chicken in nonstick shallow casserole. Melt margarine, brush chicken pieces. Bake at 375 degrees for 40 minutes. Combine juice, wine, worcestershire sauce, and garlic powder. Pour over chicken. Cover and bake 20 minutes or until tender. Remove chicken, combine corn starch and water. Add to pan juices. Cook over medium heat, stirring constantly until thickened. Remove from heat, stir in sugar substitute. Serve sauce over chicken.

Yield: 4 servings

Calories: 201 per serving
Exchanges: 4 Meat
1 Fruit

Cholesterol: 72 Mg   PRO: 28 Gm
SF: 1 Gm   CHO: 11 Gm
Sodium: 288 Mg   Fat: 5 Gm

BREAKFAST CASSEROLE

Vegetable cooking spray
3/4 lb. lean ground turkey sausage
2 cloves garlic, minced
1 cup skim milk
2 (8 oz.) cartons frozen egg substitute, thawed
1/4 cup (1 oz.) shredded, low-fat cheddar cheese
3 green onions, chopped
3/4 teaspoon dry mustard
1/4 teaspoon ground red pepper
1 (1 oz.) slice white bread, cut into 1/2" cubes
Cherry tomatoes (optional)
Green onion tops (optional)

Coat a skillet with cooking spray, place over medium heat until hot.
Add next 2 ingredients, cook until meat is browned, stirring to
crumble meat. Drain in a colander, pat dry with paper towels and set
aside. Combine milk and next 5 ingredients in a large bowl; stir well.
Add meat mixture and bread, stirring just until well blended. Pour
into an 11 x 7 x 2-inch baking dish coated with cooking spray. Cover
and chill 8 to 12 hours. Bake uncovered at 350 degrees for 50
minutes or until set and lightly browned. Garnish with tomatoes and
onions, if desired.

Yield: 6 servings

Calories: 231 per serving
Exchanges: 4 Meat

Cholesterol: 76 Mg   PRO: 27 Gm
SF: 3 Gm   CHO: 6 Gm
Sodium: 445 Mg   Fat: 11 Gm

CABBAGE ROLLS

1 large head cabbage
1 lb. ground turkey or ground turkey sausage
1/2 cup chopped onion
1/2 cup chopped celery
1/2 cup chopped bell pepper
1 1/2 cups rice, cooked
16 oz. can diced stewed tomatoes
1/4 teaspoon dill
1/4 teaspoon black pepper
1 beef boullion cube
1/2 cup water

Brown turkey with onion, celery, and bell pepper. Toss with rice and seasonings. Set aside to cool. Steam cabbage to remove leaves. Remove about 18 leaves. Lay cabbage leaf flat. Place 1/4 cup meat and rice mixture in center of leaf. Fold the two sides overlapping each other, to roll from one end to the other. Place seam side down in 13 x 9 x 2-inch pan. Heat water. Add bouillon to dissolve. Blend tomatoes and broth. Pour over cabbage rolls. Cover with aluminum foil. Bake in a 350-degree oven 1 hour.

Yield: 6 servings (3 cabbage rolls per serving)

Calories: 207 per serving
Exchanges: 3 Meat
            1/2 Bread
            2 Vegetable

Cholesterol: 53 Mg   PRO: 27 Gm
SF: 1 Gm   CHO: 18 Gm
Sodium: 418 Mg   Fat: 3 Gm

CHILI CON CARNE

1 tablespoon diet margarine
1 cup chopped onions
1 garlic clove, pressed
2 lbs. ground turkey or chicken
4 teaspoons chili powder
2 teaspoons cumin
1 teaspoon salt
1 teaspoon oregano
1 teaspoon paprika
1/4 teaspoon ground red pepper
1/4 teaspoon freshly ground pepper
1 can (13 3/4 or 14 1/2 oz.) beef broth (defatted)
1 can (28 oz.) crushed tomatoes
2 cans (15 or 16 oz. each) kidney beans, drained and rinsed

In dutch oven, melt margarine, add onions and garlic. Saute' until onions are translucent. Add ground turkey, chili powder, cumin, salt, oregano, paprika, peppers, beef broth, and tomatoes. Simmer 30 minutes. Add kidney beans and simmer 10 minutes more. (Chili improves in flavor if refrigerated for a day and then reheated).

Yield: 10 servings

Calories: 206 per serving
Exchanges: 2 Meat
1 Bread
1 Vegetable

Cholesterol: 58 Mg   PRO: 17 Gm
SF: 1 Gm   CHO: 21 Gm
Sodium: 648 Mg   Fat: 6 Gm

EASY RED BEANS AND RICE

1 lb. ground turkey sausage
1/4 cup chopped bell pepper
1/4 cup chopped celery
1/4 cup chopped green onion
1/4 teaspoon each: Garlic powder
                        Oregano
                        Red pepper
                        Black pepper

1 can red beans
1 can beef broth
2 cups Minute rice

Brown ground turkey sausage.   Add vegetables, cook 2-3 minutes.
Stir in dry seasonings.   Add broth and beans.   Bring to a rolling boil.
Add rice, cover, let set 5-10 minutes.

Yield: 6 servings (1 1/2 cups)

Calories: 308 per serving
Exchanges: 3 Meat
                1 1/2 Bread

Cholesterol: 54 Mg   PRO: 28 Gm
SF: 2 Gm   CHO: 31 Gm
Sodium: 606 Mg   Fat: 8 Gm

_____
Yield: 8 servings (1 cup)

Calories: 230 per serving
Exchanges: 2 Meat
                1 1/2 Bread

Cholesterol: 36 Mg   PRO: 21 Gm
SF: 1 Gm   CHO: 23 Gm
Sodium: 454 Mg   Fat: 6 Gm

EGGPLANT DRESSING

2 medium eggplants, peeled and boiled until tender
3 tablespoons diet margarine
2 cups chopped onion
1 pound ground turkey, browned
1/2 cup green pepper
1/2 cup celery
6 tablespoons parsley
1 clove garlic
1/2 cup green onion
2 cups rice, cooked
1/2 cup water
4 slices liteline cheese

Mix all ingredients except cheese. Season with Mrs. Dash. Bake in 350-degree oven 25-30 minutes. The last 5 minutes, lay liteline cheese on top.

Yield: 8 servings

Calories: 212
Exchanges: 2 Meat
          1/2 Bread
          2 Vegetable
          1 Fat

Cholesterol: 36 Mg   PRO: 18 Gm
S.F: 3 Gm   CHO: 17 Gm
Sodium: 286 Mg   Fat: 8 Gm

OVEN JAMBALAYA

21 oz. beef consomme' (2 cans)
21 oz. onion soup (2 cans)
1 cup fresh mushrooms
1 lb. ground turkey sausage
1/2 cup bell pepper, chopped
1 medium onion, chopped
3 cups long grain raw rice
3 ribs celery, chopped
10 oz. water
1 clove garlic, minced
1/2 teaspoon creole seasoning

Combine all ingredients in a casserole dish. Bake at 375 degrees for 40 minutes. Stir occasionally. Bake uncovered at 300 degrees for about 20 minutes or until all liquid is absorbed into rice.

Yield: 8 servings

Calories: 338 per serving
Exchanges: 1 1/2 Meat
                    2 1/2 Bread
                    1 Vegetable

Cholesterol: 36 Mg   PRO: 11 Gm
SF: 2 Gm   CHO: 60 Gm
Sodium: 651 Mg   Fat: 6 Gm

ROAST TURKEY BREAST

1 fresh turkey breast, 2 pounds
Mrs. Dash
Black pepper

Remove skin from turkey. Rub breast with generous amount of seasonings. Cover in dutch oven or use a baking bag to retain moisture. Bake at 325 degrees approximately 1 to 1 1/2 hours.

Yield: 4 servings

Calories: 148 per serving
Exchanges: 4 Meat

Cholesterol: 72 Mg   PRO: 28 Gm
SF: 1 Gm   CHO: 0 Gm
Sodium: 59 Mg   Fat: 4 Gm

SPICY PASTA BAKE

4 oz. broken spagetti
1 pound turkey breakfast sausage
1 cup sliced fresh mushrooms
1/2 cup chopped onion
1 glove garlic, minced
1 can tomatoes (10 oz.), cut up
1/2 (6 oz.) can tomato paste
1 teaspoon Italian seasoning, crushed
Nonstick cooking spray
1 cup shredded mozzarella cheese (4 oz.)
2 tablespoons grated parmesan or romano cheese

Cook spagetti in boiling water 10 to 12 minutes and drain.

Meanwhile, in a large skillet, cook turkey sausage, mushrooms, onion, and garlic until meat is brown and onion is tender. Drain fat. Stir in undrained tomatoes, tomato paste, and Italian seasoning. Spray a 9-inch quiche dish with nonstick cooking spray. Place half the spagetti in the bottom of the dish; top with half the mozzarella and half the sausage mixture. Repeat layers. Cover loosely with foil. Bake in a 350-degree oven for 25 to 30 minutes or until heated through. Top with parmesan. Let stand 10 minutes. Cut wedges to serve.

Yield: 6 servings

Calories: 285 per serving
Exchanges: 3 Meat
            1 Bread
            1 Vegetable

Cholesterol: 81 Mg   PRO: 26 Gm
SF: 3 Gm   CHO: 25 Gm
Sodium: 400 Mg   Fat: 9 Gm

STUFFED PEPPER

6 large green peppers
1 large onion, minced
3 tomatoes, peeled and chopped
1 cup cooked rice
1 lb. ground turkey
Nonstick vegetable spray
1/4 teaspoon pepper
1/2 cup bread crumbs

Cut off top of each pepper; remove seeds. Cover peppers in boiling water and cook for 3-4 minutes; drain. Cook turkey and onions in vegetable spray. Add tomatoes; simmer for 8-10 minutes. Add remaining ingredients except bread crumbs. Stir. Stuff peppers with turkey mixture and place in shallow baking dish. Top with bread crumbs. Bake at 350 degrees for 20-25 minutes.

Yield: 6 servings

Calories: 174
Exchanges: 2 1/2 Meat
             2 Vegetable
             1/2 Bread

Cholesterol: 47 Mg   PRO: 9 Gm
SF: 2 Gm   CHO: 21 Gm
Sodium: 122 Mg   Fat: 6 Gm

TURKEY AND MUSHROOM STUFFED SHELLS

8 large pasta shells
1 (16 oz.) can tomatoes, cut up
1/4 cup dry red wine
2 tablespoons tomato paste
1 tablespoon corn starch
1/2 teaspoon dried oregano, crushed
3/4 pound lean ground turkey
2 cups sliced fresh mushrooms
1 medium onion, chopped (1/2 cup)
1/2 cup chopped green pepper
1/4 teaspoon garlic powder
1/4 cup grated parmesan cheese

Cook pasta according to package directions until tender. Drain. Rinse with cold water, drain again.

In a medium saucepan, combine undrained tomatoes, wine, tomato paste, corn starch, and oregano. Cook and stir until thickened and bubbly. Set aside.

In a skillet, cook meat, mushrooms, onion, green pepper, and garlic until meat is browned; drain. Stir in 1/2 teaspoon salt. Place in 10 x 6 x 2-inch baking dish. Top with sauce. Sprinkle with parmesan. Bake covered in 350-degree oven 20 to 25 minutes or until heated through.

Yield: 4 servings

Calories: 271 per serving
Exchanges: 2 Meat
            1 1/2 Bread
            2 Vegetable

Cholesterol: 36 Mg   PRO: 16 Gm
SF: 2 Gm   CHO: 36 Gm
Sodim: 349 Mg   Fat: 7 Gm

CHEESY BEEF AND NOODLES

1 cup noodles
1 cup low-fat cottage cheese
1 pound ground round, browned and drained
1 cup mozzarella cheese with part skim milk
6 spring onions, chopped
1/3 cup canned mushrooms
2 cups tomato sauce
1 teaspoon pepper
1 teaspoon garlic powder
2 tablespoons margarine
1 cup plain low-fat yogurt

Boil noodles until tender, approximately 9 minutes. Drain well.
Alternate layers of noodles, cottage cheese, ground round, and
mozzarella in 3-quart baking dish. Mix thoroughly onions,
mushrooms, tomato sauce, pepper, garlic powder, and yogurt. Pour
mixture over layers in baking dish. Cover and bake at 350 degrees
for 45 minutes.

Yields: 8 servings

Calories: 303 per serving
Exchanges: 2 Meat
             1 Bread
             1 Vegetable
             1 Fat

Cholesterol: 94 Mg   PRO: 22 Gm
SF: 6 Gm   CHO: 20 Gm
Sodium: 254 Mg   Fat: 15 Gm

FRIED RICE

1 cup raw rice
2 tablespoons lite soy sauce
2 tablespoons margarine
1 1/2 cups vegetables-carrots, onions, bell pepper, celery,
  mushrooms, broccoli, cauliflower, or cabbage.)
1/2 cup starch: peas and corn
1 cup leftover rump roast, turkey, chicken, boiled shrimp,
  or a combination
1/4 cup roasted peanuts, shelled

Cook rice in 1 1/2 cups water with 2 tablespoons soy sauce added for
12 minutes. Set aside. Melt margarine in a skillet or wok. Stir-fry
vegetables until tender but crisp. Add meat and rice, toss until
thoroughly mixed. When serving, sprinkle with a few peanuts.

Yield: 8 servings

Calories: 216 per serving
Exchanges: 1 Meat
           1 Bread
           1/2 Fat

Cholesterol: 11 Mg   PRO: 12 Gm
SF: less than 1 Gm   CHO: 24 Gm
Sodium: 371 Mg   Fat: 8 Gm

OLD-FASHIONED BEEF STEW

1 1/4 lbs. boneless beef round steak, cut into 1-inch cubes, trim fat
1 tablespoon diet margarine
1 teaspoon worcestershire sauce
2 bay leaves
1 clove garlic, minced
1/2 teaspoon paprika
8 medium carrots, quartered
4 small potatoes, peeled and quartered
4 small onions, quartered
1 tablespoon corn starch

In dutch oven, brown beef in margarine. Add next 4 ingredients, 1 1/2 cups hot water, and 1/4 teaspoon pepper. Cook covered 1 1/4 hours; stir often. Remove bay leaves, add vegetables. Cook covered 30 to 45 minutes. Drain, reserve liquid, skim fat. Add water to liquid to equal 1 1/4 cups, return to dutch oven. Combine corn starch and 1/4 cup cold water, stir into hot liquid. Cook and stir until thickened; stir in beef and vegetables. Heat thoroughly.

Yield: 8 servings

Calories: 192 per serving
Exchanges: 2 Meat
             1/2 Bread
             1 Vegetable

Cholesterol: 46 Mg   PRO: 19 Gm
SF: 3 Gm   CHO: 11 Gm
Sodium: 87 Mg   Fat: 8 Gm

PEPPER STEAK

1 lb. round steak
2 teaspoons lite soy sauce
1 teaspoon garlic powder
2 cups green peppers, sliced in strips
2 cups celery, cut diagonally
1 cup chopped green onions
4 teaspoons vegetable oil
1/4 cup water
1 tablespoon corn starch

Trim all fat from steak, cut across grain in slices about 1-inch by 1/4-inch. Add soy sauce and garlic, stir and set aside. Prepare vegetables. Heat half of oil until very hot in large skillet. Add vegetables and stir-fry 2 minutes, remove from skillet to warm pan. Add remaining oil to skillet, heat, add steak and stir-fry 2 minutes. Mix corn starch with water, add to steak. Cook, stirring constantly, until thickened. Add vegetables. Mix thoroughly.

Serving suggestion: Serve over brown rice.

Yield: 4 servings

Calories: 348 per serving
Exchanges: 4 Meat
             1 Vegetable

Cholesterol: 91 Mg   PRO: 38 Gm
SF: 7 Gm   CHO: 13 Gm
Sodium: 300 Mg   Fat: 16 Gm

STEAK-VEGETABLE POCKETS

3/4 lb. boneless beef top round steak
Nonstick vegetable spray coating
3/4 cup thinly sliced squash
3/4 cup thinly sliced broccoli
1 small carrot, thinly sliced
1 small onion, sliced
1/2 green pepper, cut into strips
1 tablespoon cooking oil
8 pea pods, halved crosswise
6 fresh mushrooms, sliced
1 small tomato, chopped
3 tablespoons lite soy sauce
1 1/2 teaspoons corn starch
4 pita bread rounds, halved

Thinly slice beef into bite-size strips. Spray a wok or large skillet with nonstick spray coating. Heat wok or skillet over high heat. Add squash, broccoli, carrot, onion, and green pepper; stir-fry for 7 minutes. Add pea pods, mushrooms, and tomato; stir-fry for 2 minutes. Remove vegetables. Add cooking oil, heat over high heat. Stir-fry beef in hot oil 3 minutes. Combine 1/4 cup cold water and soy sauce, blend in corn starch. Add to wok or skillet. Cook and stir until bubbly. Return vegetables to wok, heat thoroughly. Spoon mixture into halved pita bread rounds. This recipe is a meal within itself!

Yield: 4 servings

Calories: 393 per serving
Exchanges: 3 Meat
2 Bread
2 Vegetable

Cholesterol: 68 Mg   PRO: 29 Gm
SF: 5 Gm   CHO: 40 Gm
Sodium: 295 Mg   Fat: 13 Gm

STIR-FRY BEEF AND VEGETABLES

16 oz. round steak, cut in small cubes
2 tablespoons olive oil
1 onion, chopped
1 rib celery, chopped
1/2 large bell pepper, chopped
3 green onions, chopped
1/2 large cabbage sliced in thin strips
2 tablespoons lite soy sauce

Brown cubed round steak in 2 tablespoons olive oil. Add onion, celery, and bell pepper. Cook until onions are transparent. Add cabbage. Cook 2-3 minutes. Add soy sauce, cover, and let stand 5 minutes. Serve over hot rice.

Yield: 6 servings

Calories: 217 per serving
Exchanges: 2 Meat
           1 Vegetable

Cholesterol: 44 Mg   PRO: 18 Gm
SF: 7 Gm   CHO: 7 Gm
Sodium: 460 Mg   Fat: 13 Gm

BAR-B-QUE PORK SKEWERS

2 (1/2 lb.) pork tenderloins
1/4 cup lemon juice
2 tablespoons reduced calorie catsup
2 tablespoons molasses
1 tablespoon vegetable oil
1/2 teaspoon garlic powder
1 teaspoon Mrs. Dash
1/2 teaspoon ground cumin
1/4 teaspoon salt
Vegetable cooking spray

Trim fat from tenderloins. Cut tenderloins into 6" x 1/4"-thick strips. Thread strips onto 4 (8") wood skewers. Combine next 8 ingredients in a large dish; stir well. Place skewers in marinade, turning to coat. Cover and marinate in refrigerator 3 hours, turning skewers occasionally.

Place skewers on a rack coated with vegetable cooking spray. Place rack on a broiler pan. Broil 6 inches from heat about 3 minutes or until done.

Yield: 4 servings

Calories: 275 per serving
Exchanges: 4 Meat
             1 Fruit
             1 Fat

Cholesterol: 105 Mg   PRO: 37 Gm
SF: 4 Gm   CHO: 9 Gm
Sodium: 253 Mg   Fat: 15 Gm

ONION-SMOTHERED PORK TENDERLOINS

2 (1/2 lb). pork tenderloins
Vegetable cooking spray
2 teaspoons diet margarine, melted
2 cups diced onion
1 teaspoon Mrs. Dash
1/4 teaspoon salt
1/4 teaspoon pepper

Trim fat from tenderloins. Cut a lengthwise slit down center of each tenderloin about 2/3 of the way through the meat. Place tenderloins in opposite directions side by side on a rack that is coated with vegetable cooking spray. Place the rack in a shallow roasting pan.

Coat a large skillet with cooking spray, add margarine and place over medium heat until hot. Add onion, and saute' until tender, stirring frequently. Add seasonings stirring well. Spread onion mixture evenly over tenderloins. Bake at 400 degrees for 40 minutes or until done.

Yield: 4 servings

Calories: 210 per serving
Exchanges: 3 Meat
            1 Vegetable

Cholesterol: 84 Mg   PRO: 33 Gm
SF: 3 Gm   CHO: 6 Gm
Sodium: 221 Mg   Fat: 6 Gm

PORK CUTLETS WITH TOMATO GRAVY

6 lean pork cutlets (each about 3/4-inch thick)
1 (8 oz.) can tomato sauce
1/2 cup sliced mushrooms
1 small green pepper cut into 1/4-inch strips
1/2 teaspoon Italian herbs
1/4 cup chopped green onions
1 (8 oz.) package skim mozzarella cheese, cut into 6 slices
Nonstick vegetable cooking spray

Trim all visible fat from pork cutlets. In 12-inch skillet over medium heat, cook pork cutlets in nonstick cooking spray until brown on both sides. Add tomato sauce, mushrooms, green pepper, onion, and Italian herbs. Reduce heat to low. Cover and simmer 30 minutes or until meat is fork tender. Top each cutlet with cheese slices. Cook 5 more minutes.

Yield: 6 servings

Calories: 272 per serving
Exchanges: 4 Meat
                    1/2 Vegetable
                    1 Fat

Cholesterol: 126 Mg   PRO: 28 Gm
SF: 7 Gm   CHO: 4 Gm
Sodium: 398 Mg   Fat: 16 Gm

VEGETABLE PORK SKILLET

4 pork cutlets 1/2-inch thick (1 lb. total)
1 tablespoon cooking oil
2 medium onions, thinly sliced and separated into rings
1 (10 oz.) can tomatoes, cut in quarters
3/4 cup water
2 teaspoons paprika
1/2 teaspoon garlic powder
1/2 teaspoon celery powder
3 medium potatoes, sliced
1 small green pepper, cut in strips

Trim fat. Cook cutlets in oil until browned, and remove from skillet. Cook onions in skillet until tender; drain. Add tomatoes with juice, water, paprika, garlic powder, and celery seed. Return cutlets to skillet. Bring dish to a boil. Reduce heat, cover and simmer 10-15 mintues. Add potatoes and green pepper. Cover and simmer 20 minutes until no pink remains in pork. Serve immediately.

Yield: 4 servings

Calories: 411 per serving
Exchanges: 4 Meat
           1 Bread
           1 Vegetable

Cholesterol: 108 Mg   PRO: 35 Gm
SF: 4 Gm   CHO: 34 Gm
Sodium: 182 Mg   Fat: 15 Gm

ROAST QUAIL

6 quail
1/3 cup diet margarine
1 teaspoon worcestershire sauce
Dash of garlic powder
2 slices lemon
1/3 cup flour
1/8 teaspoon salt
Pepper to taste

Salt and pepper birds. Flour lightly. Brown on top of stove in margarine. Add 1/4 cup water, worcestershire, garlic, and lemon. Cover roaster and cook in 350-degree oven for 1 1/4 hours. Baste birds often. Water may be added if necessary while cooking.

Yield: 6 servings

Calories: 165 per serving
Exchanges: 3 Meat
            1 Fat

Cholesterol: 88 Mg   PRO: 25 Gm
SF: 2 Gm   CHO: 5 Gm
Sodium: 199 Mg   Fat: 5 Gm

POTLUCK VENISON

2 pounds venison, cut in 2-inch cubes
1/2 cup flour
1/2 teaspoon pepper
1/2 teaspoon salt
1/4 cup corn oil
2 cups carrots, sliced
1 large can tomatoes
1/4 teaspoon garlic powder
1 large onion, quartered
2 ribs celery, sliced
2 potatoes, cubed

Mix salt and pepper with flour. Coat venison in flour mixture. Brown into 1/4 cup oil. Drain. Place meat and remaining ingredients in slow cooker for 6-8 hours on low.

Yield: 8 servings

Calories: 294 per serving
Exchanges: 4 Meat
          1 Vegetable
          1 Bread

Cholesterol: 74 Mg   PRO: 32 Gm
SF: 1 Gm   CHO: 19 Gm
Sodium: 178 Mg   Fat: 10 Gm

VENISON TENDERLOIN

2 pounds venison tenderloin
1 cup lite Italian dressing
1/2 teaspoon pepper
1 cup chopped onion
1 cup chopped celery
2 large carrots sliced diagonally

Marinate venison overnight in Italian dressing and pepper. Pound venison with mallet until tender and flat, saving Italian dressing drippings. Layer onions, celery, and carrots. Roll into a jelly-roll. Tie with string, wrapping the meat securely. Brush with Italian dressing and smoke until done.

Yield: 8 servings

Calories: 185 per serving
Exchange: 4 Meat
             1 Vegetable

Cholesterol: 74 Mg   PRO: 29 Gm
SF: less than 1 Gm   CHO: 6 Gm
Sodium: 338 Mg   Fat: 5 Gm

BAR-B-Q SAUCE

1 (8 oz.) can tomato sauce
1/4 cup fresh lemon juice
1 tablespoon brown sugar
2 tablespoons vinegar
1 teaspoon worcestershire sauce
1 teaspoon prepared mustard
Dash pepper
Dash red pepper
1/8 teaspoon garlic powder

Combine ingredients in a saucepan. Bring to a boil. Cover and simmer 15-20 minutes on low heat. Excellent to marinate chicken or meats overnight and grill.

Yield: 1 1/3 cups

Calories: 12 per 2 tablespoon serving
Exchanges: Free

Cholesterol: 0 Mg   PRO: 0 Gm
SF: 0 Gm   CHO: 3 Gm
Sodium: 24 Mg   Fat: 0 Gm

BROWN GRAVY

2 cups defatted beef broth
2 tablespoons corn starch
Dash salt
Dash pepper

Save leftover meat broth and place in refrigerator several hours. Skim fat from broth. Place defatted broth over low heat, adding 2 tablespoons corn starch until thickened. Season to taste.

Yield: 2 tablespoons=1 serving

Calories: 2 per serving
Exchanges: Free

Cholesterol: 0 Mg   PRO: 0 Gm
SF: 0 Gm   CHO: 0 Gm
Sodium: 55 Mg   Fat: 0 Gm

FAT FREE ROUX

Place 1 cup flour in cast iron skillet or dutch oven.   Bake at 400 degrees until dark brown.   Stir occasionally.

MICROWAVE METHOD:

Place 1 cup flour in pyrex casserole dish.   Microwave high for 2 minutes; stir well.   Repeat at 2-minute intervals, stirring well until flour is dark brown.

Yield: 1 cup

Serving: 2 1/2 Tablespoons

Calories: 7 2
Exchanges: 1 Bread

Cholesterol: 0 M g   PRO: 3 Gm
SF: 0 Gm   CHO: 15 Gm
Sodium: 0 Mg   Fat: 0 Gm

VEGETABLE SAUCE

12 oz. V-8 (vegetable cocktail) juice
1 tablespoon corn starch
1/4 cup chopped onion
1/4 cup chopped celery
1 tablespoon diet margarine

Saute' chopped onion and celery in margarine until tender. Set aside. Add V-8 juice to saucepan over low heat. Add 1 tablespoon corn starch, mixing well. Cook quickly, stirring constantly until thickened.

Use over rice and meats as a gravy.

Calories: 12=2   tablespoons
Exchanges: Free

Cholesterol: 0 Mg   PRO: less than 1 Gm
SF: 0 Gm   CHO: less than 1 Gm
Sodium : 28 Mg   Fat: less than 1 Gm

WHITE SAUCE

(1 cup medium white sauce)

2 tablespoons margarine
2 tablespoons all-purpose flour
1/4 teaspoon salt
1 cup skim milk

Melt margarine in saucepan over low heat. Blend in flour, salt, and dash of white or black pepper. Add milk all at once. Cook quickly, stirring constantly until mixture thickens and bubbles.

Yield: 2 tablespoons=1 serving

Calories: 34 per serving
Exchanges: Free

Cholesterol: 1 Mg   PRO: 1 Gm
SF: less than 1 Gm   CHO: 3 Gm
Sodium: 111 Mg   Fat: 2 Gm

Vegetables *and* Starches

BRAISED CABBAGE

6 cups raw cabbage
1/2 cup green onions
Butter flavored cooking spray
Liquid smoke
Pepper

Generously spray skillet or dutch oven with butter flavored cooking spray. Heat and braise cabbage and onions. When tender, add a few drops of liquid smoke and sprinkle with pepper to taste.

Yield: 6 servings

Calories: 21 per serving
Exchanges: 1 Vegetable

Cholesterol: 0 Mg   PRO: 1 Gm
SF: 0 Gm   CHO: 4 Gm
Sodium: 12 Mg   Fat: less than 1 Gm

BROCCOLI-POTATO BAKE

4 small potatoes, peeled and diced
2 teaspoons diet margarine
1 teaspoon salt
1/4 cup skim milk
1 pkg. frozen chopped broccoli (10 oz.)
1/4 cup grated low-fat cheddar cheese (about 1 oz.)

Cook, drain, and mash potatoes with diet margarine, salt, and milk.
Preheat oven to 350 degrees.   Cook broccoli according to package
directions. Drain well. Fold into mashed potatoes.

Put in casserole sprayed with vegetable pan spray.   Sprinkle with
cheese. Bake for 10-15 minutes or until cheese melts.

Yield: 4 cups

Calories: 150 per cup
Exchanges: 1 Bread
                  1 Vegetable

Cholesterol: 9 Mg   PRO: 4 Gm
SF: 1 Gm   CHO: 29 Gm
Sodium: 124 Mg   Fat: 2 Gm

CREOLE ZUCCHINNI

3 cups zucchinni, sliced
2 tablespoons margarine
1 medium onion, chopped
1 cup sliced celery
1/4 teaspoon garlic powder
1/4 teaspoon oregano
1/8 teaspoon red and black pepper
1 (16 oz.) can diced stewed tomatoes

Saute' onion, celery, and seasonings in margarine. Add zucchinni and can of stewed tomatoes. Simmer 30 minutes.

Yield: 8 servings

Calories: 67 per serving
Exchanges: 1 Vegetable
1 Fat

Cholesterol: 0 Mg   PRO: 3 Gm
SF: less than 1 Gm   CHO: 7 Gm
Sodium: 248 Mg   Fat: 3 Gm

GREEN BEANS AND POTATOES IN CREAM SAUCE

4 cups fresh green beans
8 small new red potatoes
2 cups skim milk
2 tablespoons corn starch
2 pkgs. butter buds
Pepper to taste

Cook green beans and potatoes in large pot with 1 1/2 quarts water. Dissolve 2 pkgs. butter buds with 1 cup hot water and add to green beans. Additional water may be added if needed. Green beans and potatoes should be tender. Mix 1/4 cup skim milk with 2 tablespoons corn starch. Add this mixture to remaining skim milk. Pour skim milk mixture into green beans and potatoes. Cook until thickened to desired consistency. Add pepper to taste.

Yield: 8 servings

Calories: 100 per serving
Exchanges: 1 Bread
1 Vegetable

Cholesterol: 3 Mg   PRO: 4 Gm
SF: less than 1 Gm   CHO: 21 Gm
Sodium: 33 Mg   Fat: less than 1 Gm

HOT AND SPICY CABBAGE

2 oz. center cut smoked ham
1/2 cup chopped onions
1/2 cup chopped bell peppers
10 oz. can chopped rotel tomatoes
1/2 teaspoon sugar
4 cups cabbage, sliced
1/8 teaspoon white and black pepper
Olive oil flavored cooking spray

Stir-fry ham, onion, and bell pepper in cooking spray. Add rotel tomatoes and sugar; simmer 2-3 minutes. Add cabbage and peppers. Simmer 15 minutes.

Yield: 8 servings

Calories: 30 per serving
Exchanges: 1 Vegetable

Cholesterol: 4 Mg   PRO: 2 Gm
SF: 3 Gm   CHO: 5 Gm
sodium: 244 Mg   Fat: less than 1 Gm

OVEN-FRIED OKRA

1 1/4 cups corn meal
1/2 teaspoon salt
Pepper to taste
4 cups fresh okra
Vegetable cooking spray

Combine first 3 ingredients; set aside.

Wash okra; drain. Cut off tip and stem ends; cut okra into 1/2-inch slices. Dredge in corn meal mixture. Okra must be moist for corn meal mixture to coat well. Rinse again before dredging, if necessary.

Lightly coat a 15 x 10 x 1-inch jellyroll pan with cooking spray. Spread okra in a single layer pan. Bake at 350 degrees for 30 to 40 minutes or until crisp, stirring occasionally.

Yield: 8 servings

Calories: 104 per serving
Exchanges: 1 Bread
                     1 Vegetable

Cholesterol: 0 Mg   PRO: 4 Gm
S.F: 0 Mg   CHO: 21 Gm
Sodium: 127 Mg   Fat: less than 1 Gm

SEASONED GREENS

1 pound (4 cups) turnip, collard or mustard greens
2-3 slices lean chopped canadian bacon or 2 oz. lean ham
1 tablespoon sugar
2 cups turnips, peeled and diced
1/4 teaspoon salt

Wash greens thoroughly. Remove stems and place in large pot. Add 4 cups water, meat, sugar, and salt, if desired. Cover greens and cook 30-45 minutes.

Yield: 8-1/2 cup servings

Calories: 46 per cup
Exchanges: 1 Vegetable

Cholesterol: 4 Mg   PRO: 3 Gm
SF: less than 1 Gm   CHO: 7 Gm
Sodium: 138 Mg   Fat: less than 1 Gm

SMOTHERED SQUASH

6 medium squash
1 large onion, chopped
3 tablespoons diet margarine
*1 tablespoon sugar

Wash and cut squash in 1/4-inch round slices. Place in pot and cover with water. Cook on medium heat, covered, until squash are tender. Drain and set aside. In a nonstick skillet, add 3 tablespoons diet margarine and 1 large chopped onion. Cook until onion is tender. Add drained squash and 1 tablespoon sugar. Cook on medium-high heat, stirring frequently. Cook most of the moisture out of squash. Remove from heat and cover. Serve in 10-15 minutes.

*May use Sweet & Low

Yield: 6 servings
        1/2 cup=1 serving

Calories: 59 per serving
Exchanges: 1 Vegetable
            1 Fat

Cholesterol: 0 Mg   PRO: 1 Gm
S.F: less than 1 Gm   CHO: 7 Gm
Sodium: 60 Mg   Fat: 3 Gm

STEAMED VEGETABLE MEDLEY

1 cup fresh broccoli flowerettes
1 cup diagonally sliced carrots
1 teaspoon butter substitute

Cook broccoli and carrots in a vegetable steamer 8-10 minutes over boiling water or until crisp-tender. Remove from steamer, place in bowl and toss with 1 teaspoon butter substitute.

Yield: 4 servings

Calories: 29 per serving
Exchanges: 1 Vegetable

Cholesterol: 0 Mg   PRO: 1 Gm
SF: less than 1 Gm   CHO: 4 Gm
Sodium: 50 Mg   Fat: 1 Gm

STEWED OKRA & TOMATOES

1 (10 oz.) package frozen cut okra
1 (16 oz.) can tomatoes, chopped
1/3 cup chopped onions
2 tablespoons diet margarine
Dash salt
Pepper to taste

Combine all ingredients. Simmer on top of stove in a covered saucepan or skillet for 20-30 minutes. Check okra for desired tenderness.

Yield: 6 (1/2 cup) servings

Calories: 54 per serving
Exchanges: 1 Vegetable

Cholesterol: 0 Mg   PRO: 2 Gm
SF: less than 1 Gm   CHO: 7 Gm
Sodium: 250 Mg   Fat: 2 Gm

VEGETABLE KABOBS

2 medium yellow squash cut in 1" cubes
6 small onions
1 medium green pepper cut in 18 pieces
6 large mushrooms
6 small tommy toe tomatoes
1/2 cup diet Italian dressing

Place squash and small onions in boiling water, cooking 4-5 minutes until crisp-tender.   Drain and cool.   Combine in shallow dish all vegetables except tomatoes.   Pour dressing over vegetables; toss. Cover and marinate overnight in refrigerator.   Thread vegetables onto skewers, alternating different vegetables.   Grill 30 minutes over medium-hot coals, brushing with remaining marinade.

A touch of fresh rosemary adds to this dish.   Sprinkle on vegetables after basting.

Yield: 6 servings

Calories: 82 per serving
Exchanges: 2 Vegetable

Cholesterol: 1 Mg   PRO: 2 Gm
SF: less than 1 Gm   CHO: 14 Gm
Sodium: 170 Mg   Fat: 2 Gm

VEGETABLE SKILLET

2 cups thinly sliced yellow squash
1 cup carrots, sliced diagonally
1/2 cup chopped onion
1/2 cup bias-sliced celery
2 cups cabbage, thinly sliced
1 cup sliced mushrooms
1/2 teaspoon garlic powder
Dash pepper
2 tablespoons vegetable oil
4 tomato wedges

In large skillet, cook squash, carrots, onion, celery, cabbage, mushrooms, and garlic powder covered in hot oil over medium-high heat 4 minutes, stirring occasionally. Add tomato wedges and pepper. Cook 2 to 3 minutes or until heated through. Serve immediately.

Yield: 8 servings

Calories: 75 per serving
Exchanges: 2 Vegetable
1 Fat

Cholesterol: 0 Mg   PRO: 3 Gm
SF: less than 1 Gm   CHO: 9 Gm
Sodium: 16 Mg   Fat: 3 Gm

CANDIED SWEET POTATOES

4 medium sweet potatoes, cubed
4 teaspoons Sweet & Low brown sugar
4 tablespoons margarine
1/2 teaspoon cinnamon, if desired

Cook sweet potatoes until tender in water. Drain. Mix melted margarine, Sweet & Low brown sugar, and cinnamon. Arrange sweet potatoes in baking dish. Pour margarine mixture over potatoes. Bake uncovered at 350 degrees for 25-30 minutes.

Yield: 8 servings

Calories: 129 per serving
Exchange: 1 Bread
1 Fat

Cholesterol: 0 Mg   PRO: 1 Gm
SF: less than 1 Gm   CHO: 20 Gm
Sodium: 74 Mg   Fat: 5 Gm

CREOLE BLACKEYED PEAS

1 pound dried blackeyed peas
2 quarts water
1/2 cup chopped bell pepper
1/2 cup chopped onion
1/2 cup chopped green onions
1/2 cup chopped celery
1/4 teaspoon garlic powder
1/2 lb. center cut smoked ham
1/8 teaspoon black pepper to taste

Wash peas and soak overnight in cold water. Drain peas. Place all ingredients in large pot, add 2 quarts water. Cook at least 2 hours or until peas are tender. Additional water may need to be added.

Yield: 8 servings

Calories: 183 per serving
Exchanges: 1 Meat
            1 Bread
            1 Vegetable

Cholesterol: 15 Mg   PRO: 16 Gm
SF: less than 1 Gm   CHO: 23 Gm
Sodium: 154 Mg   Fat: 3 Gm

GRILLED CORN ON COB

3 tablespoons diet margarine, melted
1 tablespoon chives
2 teaspoons lemon juice
Dash pepper
6 ears fresh corn

Combine margarine, chives, lemon juice, and pepper in small bowl. Peel back husks from corn, removing silks. Brush corn with margarine mixture. Place husks back over corn and wrap corn in aluminum foil. Grill 45 minutes or until tender.

Yield: 6 servings

Calories: 95 per serving
Exchanges: 1 Bread
            1 Fat

Cholesterol: 0 Mg   PRO: 2 Gm
SF: less than 1 Gm   CHO: 15 Gm
Sodium: 71 Mg   Fat: 3 Gm

OVEN FRIED POTATOES

4 medium potatoes, skins on
1 tablespoon vegetable oil
1/8 teaspoon garlic powder
1/8 teaspoon onion powder
1-1 1/2 teaspoons paprika
Salt and pepper to taste

Slice potatoes lengthwise into eighths (1/8). Line shallow pan with foil. Put all ingredients into pan, tossing well to coat potatoes with oil and seasonings.

Bake at 325 degrees for 1 hour or at a higher temperature for less time, if you wish.

Yield: 4 servings

Calories: 145 per serving
Exchanges: 2 Bread
             1 Fat

Cholesterol: 0 Mg   PRO: 4 Gm
S F: less than 1 Gm   CHO: 30 Gm
Sodium: 128 Mg   Fat: 1 Gm

SOUTHERN BLACKEYED PEAS

*4 cups blackeyed peas
2 quarts water
1/4 teaspoon salt
*2 oz. lean ham, cubed

Place peas in large pot containing 2 quarts water. Add salt and lean ham. Cook approximately 1 hour or until peas are tender. Additional water may be added during cooking.

*Dried peas may be used; soak overnight or at least 6 hours in cold water.

*Canadian bacon may be substituted for ham.

Yield: 8 servings per 1/2 cup

Calories: 90 (1/2) per cup
Exchanges: 1 Bread
           1/2 Meat

Cholesterol: 6 Mg   PRO: 7 Gm
SF: less than 1 Gm   CHO: 15 Gm
Sodium: 135 Mg   Fat: less than 1 Gm

SPICY GRILLED CORN

6 ears corn, small
1 teaspoon Molly McButter
1/8 teaspoon chili powder

Prepare outdoor grill for cooking. Place unhusked corn into medium hot coals. Grill corn in the husk 7 to 10 minutes until tender. Combine Molly McButter flavored salt and chili powder. Sprinkle seasoning on husked ears of corn just before serving.

Note: To prepare corn indoors, remove husks. Over high heat, bring corn and enough water to cover to a boil. Boil 5 to 7 minutes until tender. Sprinkle with seasonings as above.

Yield: 6 servings

Calories: 97 per serving
Exchanges: 1 Bread

Cholesterol: 0 Mg   PRO: 3 Gm
SF: less than 1 Gm   CHO: 19 Gm
Sodium: 13 Mg   Fat: 1 Gm

Breads

Collun Cline Johnson ©

BANANA MUFFINS

1 1/4 cups all-purpose flour
1 cup whole wheat flour
1/3 cup granulated sugar
2 teaspoons baking powder
1/2 teaspoon baking soda
2 teaspoons cinnamon
1/2 teaspoon nutmeg
1/2 cup low-fat buttermilk
1/3 cup vegetable oil
3 ripe bananas (mashed)
*1 egg

In mixing bowl, combine all dry ingredients. In small bowl, combine remaining ingredients. Mix dry with moist ingredients stirring until all ingredients are moist. Fill paper-lined muffin tins or spray tins with nonstick vegetable spray filling 3/4 full. Bake at 375 degrees 15-20 minutes.

*May use egg substitute.

Yield: 18 muffins

Calories: 105 per muffin
Exchanges: 1 Bread
            1 Fruit

Cholesterol: 15 Mg   PRO: 2 Gm
S.F: less than 1 Gm   CHO: 22 Gm
Sodium: 34 Mg   Fat: 1 Gm

BLUEBERRY MUFFINS

1/4 cup vegetable oil
3/4 cup brown sugar
1 cup all-purpose flour
2 teaspoons baking powder
1 teaspoon baking soda
1/4 teaspoon salt
1 cup low-fat buttermilk
1/4 cup Eggbeaters
1/3 cup oat bran
1/3 cup oatmeal
1/3 cup wheat germ
1 cup blueberries

In a mixing bowl, combine dry ingredients. In small bowl, combine remaining ingredients. Mix dry with moist ingredients stirring until all ingredients are moist. Fill paper-lined muffin tins or spray tins with nonstick vegetable spray filling 3/4 full. Bake at 400 degrees 15-20 minutes.

Variation: Substitute raisins for blueberries

Yield: 12 muffins

Calories: 149 per muffin
Exchanges: 1 Bread
            1 Fruit
            1 Fat

Cholesterol: 0 Mg   PRO: 2 Gm
SF: less than 1 Gm   CHO: 24 Gm
Sodium: 134 Mg   Fat: 5 Gm

OAT BRAN MUFFINS

1/4 cup vegetable oil
3/4 cup brown sugar
1 cup all-purpose flour
2 teaspoons baking powder
1/4 teaspoon salt
1 cup low-fat buttermilk
1/4 cup Eggbeaters
1 teaspoon baking soda
1 1/4 cups oat bran
*1 cup raisins

In a mixing bowl, combine all dry ingredients. In small bowl, combine remaining ingredients. Mix dry with moist ingredients stirring until all ingredients are moist. Fill paper-lined muffin tins or spray tins with nonstick vegetable spray. Fill tins 3/4 full. Bake at 400 degrees 15-20 minutes.

*Variation: May substitute drained pineapple tidbits or chopped apple for raisins.

Yield: 18 muffins

Calories: 119 per muffin
Exchanges: 1 Bread
1/2 Fruit
1 Fat

Cholesterol: 0 Mg   PRO: 2 Gm
S.F: less than 1 Gm   CHO: 21 Gm
Sodium: 94 Mg   Fat: 3 Gm

SUGARLESS BANANA MUFFINS

1/4 cup vegetable oil
1 tablespoon Sweet & Low brown sugar
1 cup all-purpose flour
2 teaspoons baking powder
1 teaspoon baking soda
1/4 teaspoon salt
1 cup low-fat buttermilk
1/4 cup Eggbeaters
1/3 cup oat bran
1/3 cup oatmeal
1/3 cup wheat germ
1 large ripe banana (mashed)

In a mixing bowl, combine vegetable oil, brown sugar, flour, baking powder, baking soda, and salt. Add buttermilk, Eggbeaters, oat bran, oatmeal, and wheat germ. Stir lightly with a wooden spoon to moisten. Stir in banana. Fill paper-lined muffin tins or spray tins with nonstick vegetable spray filling 3/4 full. Bake at 400 degrees 20 minutes or until toothpick inserted into center comes out dry. Remove muffins from tins and cool on wire rack. These muffins freeze well.

Variation: Substitute blueberries or applesauce for bananas.

Yield: 18 muffins

Calories: 111 each
Exchanges: 1 Bread
1/2 Fat

Cholesterol: 0 Mg   PRO: 2 Gm
SF: less than 1 Gm   CHO: 19 Gm
Sodium: 134 Mg   Fat: 3 Gm

WHOLE WHEAT BANANA BREAD

1 1/4 cups all-purpose flour
1/2 cup whole wheat flour
1 teaspoon baking soda
1/4 teaspoon salt
1/2 cup sugar
1/4 cup vegetable oil
*1 egg
1 cup mashed ripe bananas (about 2 medium)
1 teaspoon vanilla extract
Vegetable cooking spray

Combine first 4 ingredients in a small bowl, stir well and set aside. Combine sugar and oil in a medium bowl and beat at medium speed of an electric mixer 2 minutes or until well blended. Add egg and beat until light and lemon colored.

With mixer running at low speed, add flour mixture alternately with bananas, beginning and ending with flour mixture. Blend well after each addition. Stir in vanilla. Pour batter into an 8 X 4 X 2-inch loaf pan coated with cooking spray; bake at 350 degrees for 45 minutes or until a wooden toothpick inserted in center comes out clean. Cool 15 minutes in pan on a wire rack; remove from pan and let cool completely on a wire rack.

Yield: 16 (1/2-inch slices)

Calories: 115 per slice
Exchanges: 1 Bread
1/2 Fruit
1/2 Fat

Cholesterol: 17 Mg   PRO: 2 Gm
SF: less than 1 Gm   CHO: 20 Gm
Sodium: 86 Mg   Fat: 3 Gm

*May use egg substitute.

BROCCOLI CORNBREAD

1 cup Eggbeaters
4 oz. low-fat cottage cheese
1 pkg. frozen chopped broccoli (thawed)
1 large onion
1 stick diet margarine, melted
Dash salt
Dash tobasco sauce
1 cup corn meal
1 cup flour
1/2 teaspoon salt
4 teaspoons baking powder
2 tablespoons sugar

Preheat oven to 350 degrees. Spray 12-inch iron skillet with
nonstick vegetable spray. Leave in oven while it is pre-heating. Mix
all ingredients. Pour into hot skillet. Bake 30-40 minutes.

Yield: 8 slices

Calories: 215 per slice
Exchanges: 2 Bread
              1 Fat

Cholesterol: 1 Mg   PRO: 9 Gm
SF: 1 Gm   CHO: 29 Gm
Sodium: 435 Mg   Fat: 7 Gm

CORNBREAD DRESSING

1 cup chopped onion
1 cup chopped celery
1/4 cup margarine
1 1/2 cups chicken broth (defatted)
5 cups crumbled cornbread
1 teaspoon salt
1/2 cup Eggbeaters
1/2 teaspoon pepper
1 teaspoon sage, if desired

Preheat oven to 350 degrees. Saute' onion and celery in margarine until tender. Combine cornbread, salt, and eggs. Mix in onion and celery. Add broth and remaining seasonings desired. Blend well and place in casserole dish sprayed with a nonstick vegetable spray. Bake at 350 degrees for 30-40 minutes.

Yield: 8-1 cup servings

Calories: 182 per serving
Exchanges: 1 Bread
1/2 Vegetable
1 Fat

Cholesterol: 2 Mg   PRO: 6 Gm
SF: 2 Gm   CHO: 26 Gm
Sodium: 586 Mg   Fat: 6 Gm

Yield: 16-1/2 cup servings

Calories: 91 per serving
Exchanges: 1 Bread
1 Fat

Cholesterol: 1 Mg   PRO: 3 Gm
SF: 1 Gm   CHO: 13 Gm
Sodium: 293 Mg   Fat: 3 Gm

OLD FASHIONED CORNBREAD

1 1/2 cups stoneground corn meal
1/2 cup flour
3 teaspoons baking powder
2 tablespoons sugar
1/4 cup vegetable oil
1/2 cup Eggbeaters
1/8 teaspoon salt
1 1/2 cups skim milk

Preheat oven to 400 degrees . Combine all ingredients and mix well. Pour into a 12-inch iron skillet which has been sprayed with a nonstick vegetable spray. Bake approximately 30 minutes or until golden brown.

Yield: 8 servings (slice)

Calories: 206 per slice
Exchanges: 2 Bread
1 Fat

Cholesterol: 2 Mg   PRO: 6 Gm
SF: 1 Gm   CHO: 32 Gm
Sodium: 90 Mg   Fat: 6 Gm

SKILLET CORNBREAD

1/2 cup all-purpose flour
1/4 cup grated bread crumbs
1 1/2 cups white corn meal
1 teaspoon salt or substitute
2 1/2 teaspoons baking powder
1/2 cup Eggbeaters
1 1/2 cups skim milk
2 tablespoons vegetable oil

Preheat oven to 400 degrees. Combine flour, bread crumbs, corn meal, salt, and baking powder. Combine Eggbeaters and milk in separate bowl. Stir egg mixture into corn meal mixture, mixing well. Place oil into 10-inch iron skillet, then place in preheated oven until oil is hot. Coat sides of skillet. Spoon mixture into hot skillet. Bake 25 minutes or until golden brown at 400 degrees. Cut cornbread into 9 pie- shaped portions.

Yield: 9 servings

Calories: 165 per serving
Exchanges: 1 1/2 Bread
                   1 Fat

Cholesterol: 3 Mg   PRO: 6 Gm
S.F: 1 Gm   CHO: 24 Gm
Sodium: 282 Mg   Fat: 5 Gm

SOUTHERN CORNBREAD

1 cup corn meal
1 cup flour
2 tablespoons sugar
1/2 teaspoon salt
4 teaspoons baking powder
1/4 cup Egg Beaters or 2 egg whites
1 cup skim milk
2 tablespoons oil (Peanut, safflower, corn)

Blend all dry ingredients. Spray 12-inch black iron skillet with Pam. Add 2 tablespoons oil and heat in oven while it preheats to 375 degrees. Add eggbeaters or egg whites with milk to mixture. Stir until blended. Pour into hot skillet and bake 20-25 minutes.

Yield: 8 servings

Calories: 167 per slice
Exchanges: 2 Bread
             1 Fat

Cholesterol: 0 Mg   PRO: 5 Gm
SF: 1 Gm   CHO: 30 Gm
Sodium: 150 Mg   Fat: 3 Gm

*This recipe is calculated for eggbeaters.

HOMEMADE FRENCH BREAD

3 cups all-purpose flour
1 cup lukewarm water
1 package yeast
1 1/2 teaspoons salt
2 tablespoons corn meal
Butter flavored nonstick vegetable spray

Combine yeast with water. Let stand for 5 minutes. Blend flour and salt, mix with liquid and knead 8-10 minutes. Place dough into bowl that has been sprayed with nonstick vegetable spray. Cover and allow to rise (free from drafts), 45 minutes. Spray cookie sheet with nonstick vegetable spray, sprinkle with cornmeal, set aside. Punch down dough. Divide into equal portions, roll out into rectangles and roll up length and seal. Pinch the 3 rolls together at one end and braid, seal the end of the braid by pinching again. Place braid on cookie sheet. Bake in preheated 375 degree oven for 25-30 minutes.

Yield: 12 slices

Calories: 104 per slice
Exchanges: 1 1/2 Bread

Cholesterol: 0 Mg   PRO: 3 Gm
SF: less than 1 Gm   CHO: 23 Gm
Sodium: 245 Mg   Fat: 0 Gm

SOUTHERN BISCUITS

2 cups all-purpose flour
4 teaspoons baking powder
1/2 teaspoon salt
1 tablespoon sugar
6 tablespoons margarine
3/4 cup 2% milk

Mix together first 4 ingredients. Add margarine and cut until about consistency of corn meal. Add milk and mix in with fork. On floured cutting board, knead gently, turning over several times. Roll with dusted rolling pin to 1/2-inch thickness. Cut to desired size with a glass. Bake with sides touching on ungreased cookie sheet on high shelf in oven at 450 degrees for about 10-12 minutes.

Yield: 16 biscuits

Calories: 96 per biscuit
Exchanges: 1 Bread
              1 Fat

Cholesterol: less than 1 Mg   PRO: 1 Gm
SF: less than 1 Gm   CHO: 14 Gm
Sodium: 116 Mg   Fat: 4 Gm

YEAST BISCUITS

1 pkg. yeast
1/4 cup water
3 cups all-purpose flour
3/4 cup non fat dry milk
1/4 teaspoon salt
3/4 teaspoon baking powder
2 tablespoons sugar
1 stick corn oil margarine
Butter flavored nonstick vegetable spray

Combine yeast with water. Let stand 5 minutes. Blend dry ingredients. Cut in margarine. Gradually add liquid and knead 1-2 minutes. Roll out to 1/2-inch thickness and cut 18 biscuits. Place in pan that has been generously sprayed with butter flavored nonstick vegetable spray. Allow biscuits to rise 30-35 minutes before baking. Bake in a 450- degree preheated oven 8-10 minutes.

FOOD PROCESSOR METHOD:

Combine yeast with water. Combine all dry ingredients into processor with dough blade. Pulse to mix. Cut margarine into 4 chunks and put in processor bowl. Pulse several times to cut into flour. Turn machine on. Add liquid. Processor will work it into a ball. Stop machine. Follow above directions for rolling out.

Yield: 18 biscuits

Calories: 129=1 biscuit
Exchanges: 1 Bread
             1 Fat

Cholesterol: less than 1 Mg   PRO: 2 Gm
SF: 1 Gm   CHO: 19 Gm
Sodium: 75 Mg   Fat: 5 Gm

OAT BRAN PIZZA CRUST

1 package dry yeast
1/4 cup warm water
2 tablespoons honey
2 cups all-purpose flour
1/4 cup oat bran
1/2 cup regular oats, uncooked
1/2 teaspoon salt
1/3 cup warm water

Dissolve yeast in 1/4 cup warm water, let stand 5 minutes. Stir in honey. Combine flour, oats, and salt in a large bowl. Add yeast mixture and 1/3 cup warm water to flour mixture, mixing until a soft dough forms. Turn dough out onto a lightly floured surface and knead until smooth and elastic (about 8 to 10 minutes). Place in a bowl that has been coated with cooking spray, turning to grease top. Cover and let rise in a warm place (85 degrees), free from drafts, 1 1/2 hours or until double in bulk. Punch dough down. Pat dough onto a 14-inch pizza pan that has been coated with cooking spray.

Yield: 1 crust (8 servings)

Calories: 124 per serving
Exchanges: 2 Bread

Cholesterol: 0 Mg   PRO: 4 Gm
SF: less than 1 Gm   CHO: 27 Gm
Sodium: 145 Mg   Fat: 0 Gm

Desserts

SUGAR FREE CHOCOLATE PECAN BROWNIES

2 tablespoons cocoa plus 1 tablespoon oil
1/3 cup margarine, melted
2 tablespoons liquid sweetener
2 teaspoons vanilla
2/3 cup pecans
1/2 cup eggbeaters
1 cup cake flour
1/2 teaspoon salt
1/2 teaspoon baking powder

Mix cocoa and oil. Add melted margarine, sweetener, eggbeaters, vanilla, and pecans. Blend all dry ingredients. Stir in liquid mixture. Pour into an 8 x 8-inch square pan. Smooth batter. Preheat oven to 325 degrees. Bake 20-25 minutes. Cut into 16 2-inch squares.

Yield: 16 pieces

Calories: 95 per square
Exchanges: 1/2 Bread
           1 Fat

Cholesterol: 0 Mg   PRO: 2 Gm
SF: less than 1 Gm   CHO: 6 Gm
Sodium: 117 Mg   Fat: 7 Gm

SUGAR-FREE COOKIES

Cook 2 cups raisins in 2 cups water until almost dry.

ADD: 1 cup unsweetened applesauce
2 eggs
1 pkg Sweet & Low (3 1/3 teaspoons)
3/4 cup vegetable oil
1/2 teaspoon salt
2 cups all-purpose flour
1 teaspoon cinnamon
1 teaspoon baking soda
1/2 cup chopped nuts (optional)

Mix all ingredients and bake in a 9 X 13-inch pan, greased and floured, at 350 degrees for 45 minutes.

Yield: 76 cookies

Calories: 2 cookies=83
Exchanges: 1/2 Bread
1 Fat

Cholesterol: 11 Mg   PRO: 0 Gm
SF: Less than 1 Gm   CHO: 10 Gm
Sodium: 48 Mg   Fat: 4 Gm

HEAVENLY PINEAPPLE CAKE

1 (8 oz.) can unsweetened crushed pineapple, undrained
6 eggs, separated
1/2 cup sugar
2 cups sifted cake flour
1 tablespoon baking powder
1/2 teaspoon salt
1 teaspoon almond extract
1/2 teaspoon cream of tartar

Drain pineapple, reserving juice. Add water to juice to measure 3/4 cup and set aside. Beat egg yolks at high speed with electric mixer until thick and lemon colored. Add 1/2 cup sugar and pineapple juice mixture and beat an additional 2 minutes. Combine flour, baking powder, and salt. Add to egg mixture, mixing well, and stir in almond extract. Beat egg whites (at room temperature) and cream of tartar until soft peaks form. Gently fold egg white mixture and crushed pineapple into batter. Spoon batter into an ungreased 10-inch tube pan. Bake at 350 degrees for 50 to 55 minutes or until top of cake springs back when lightly touched. Invert cake; cool 1 hour or until completely cooled before removing from pan.

Yield: 16 servings

Calories: 118 per serving
Exchanges: 1 Bread
            1/2 Fruit
            1/2 Fat

Cholesterol: 102 Mg   PRO: 5 Gm
SF: less than 1 Gm   CHO: 20 Gm
Sodium: 87 Mg   Fat: 2 Gm

STRAWBERRY CHEESECAKE

2/3 cup graham cracker crumbs
3 tablespoons diet margarine

Melt margarine in 8" X 8" dish. Add crumbs. Mix and press. Bake at 350 degrees for 8 minutes. Cool.

1 package lemon nutrasweet Jello
1 cup low-fat cottage cheese
1 package Dream Whip (prepared as directed)
5-6 pkgs. Equal (or to taste)

Dissolve jello with 1 cup hot water. Add 3/4 cup cold water and Equal. Refrigerate until slightly congealed. Blend cottage cheese in blender until smooth. Add the thickened Jello and milk. Add this mixture to prepared Dream Whip. Mix well and pour over crumbs.

TOPPING: 2 cups fresh or frozen strawberries
                  2 tablespoons low calorie strawberry jelly
                  2-3 teaspoons water
                  2 packages Equal

Mix water, Equal and topping. Add sliced strawberries. Top each serving of cheesecake with topping.

Yield: 9 servings

Calories: 149 per Serving
Exchanges: 1/2 Bread
               1/2 Fruit
               2 Fat

Cholesterol: 2 Mg   PRO: 5 Gm
SF: 2 Gm   CHO: 12 Gm
Sodium: 221 Mg   Fat: 9 Gm

SUGAR-FREE APPLESAUCE LOAF CAKE

3 cups all-purpose flour
15 pkgs. Sweet & Low
2 teaspoons soda
2 teaspoons baking powder
2 teaspoons cinnamon
1/4 teaspoon salt
2 cups unsweetened applesauce
1 cup vegetable oil
4 eggs
1/2 cup raisins
1/2 cup chopped nuts (optional)

Mix all ingredients. DO NOT GREASE PAN. Bake at 350 degrees for 45 minutes. DO NOT USE ELECTRIC MIXER. Mix by hand. May be baked in bundt pan. May be cut into slices, wrapped individually and frozen.

Yield: 16 slices

Calories: 223   per slice
Exchanges: 3 Fat
                    1 1/2 Bread

Cholesterol: 68 Mg   PRO: 1 Gm
SF: 2 Gm   CHO: 21 Gm
Sodium: 155 Mg   Fat: 15 Gm

HEAVEN-LIGHT LEMON PIE

2 egg whites
1/2 teaspoon vinegar
1/2 teaspoon vanilla
3 tablespoons sugar
*2 beaten eggs

1/4 cup lemon juice
1/4 cup sugar
1 tablespoon margarine
2 pkgs. whipped lite topping
1 cup cold water

Spray a 9-inch pie plate with nonstick spray coating. In a small mixing bowl, combine egg whites, vinegar, 1/2 teaspoon vanilla, and dash salt; beat with electric mixer on high speed until soft peaks form. Gradually add 3 tablespoons sugar, beating to stiff peaks. Spread meringue over bottom and sides of pie plate to form a crust. Bake in 325-degree oven 25 minutes or until lightly browned. Cool.

Combine eggs, lemon juice, 1/4 cup sugar, and margarine. Cook and stir over low heat until slightly thickened. Spread 1/4 of mixture over meringue. Prepare dessert topping mix according to package directions, using water and remaining vanilla. Spoon half the whipped topping into pie plate. Fold together remaining whipped topping and remaining lemon mixture. Spoon into pie plate. Cover, chill several hours.

Yield: 8 slices

Calories: 118 per slice
Exchanges: 1 Bread
             1 Fat

Cholesterol: 68 Mg   PRO: 2 Gm
SF: 4 Gm   CHO: 14 Gm
Sodium: 59 Mg   Fat: 6 Gm

*May substitute eggbeaters to eliminate cholesterol.

SUGARLESS APPLE PIE

1 (6 oz.) can apple juice concentrate
2 tablespoons corn starch
4 apples
1/2 can water
1/2 teaspoon apple pie spice

Mix all ingredients. Cook until thick. Slice apples into raw crust. Pour mixture over apples. Cover with top crust. Bake at 350 degrees for 45 minutes. Apples may be sprinkled with one package of Sweet & Low, if desired.

This pie may be made without the crust to save calories. Pour mixture over apples in pie pan.

Yield: 8 slices

Calories: 60 per slice w/o crust
Exchanges: 1 1/2 Fruit

Cholesterol: 0 Mg   PRO: less than 1 Gm
SF: 0 Gm   CHO: 15 Gm
Sodium: 1 Mg   Fat: 0 Gm

Calories: 256 per slice with crust
Exchanges: 2 Bread
            1 1/2 Fruit
            2 Fat

Cholesterol: 0 Mg   PRO: 4 Gm
SF: 2 Gm   CHO: 51 Gm
Sodium: 261 Mg   Fat: 4 Gm

*Calories calculated using Mama Bays' Pie Crust. See Page 211.

APPLE-PINEAPPLE BAKE

3 medium baking apples
1/2 cup unsweetened crushed pineapple, drained.
   (Reserve juice)
1/2 teaspoon cinnamon
1 1/2 teaspoons sugar
1/3 cup reserved pineapple juice
2 tablespoons chopped walnuts or pecans
Vegetable cooking spray

Preheat oven to 350 degrees. Peel and slice apples into 8- inch pie plate sprayed with vegetable cooking spray. Spoon pineapple over apples. Sprinkle with cinnamon and sugar. Pour juice over fruit. Sprinkle nuts evenly over top. Bake for 40 minutes. May be served warm or chilled.

Yield: 6 servings

Calories: 53 per serving
Exchanges: 1 Fruit

Cholesterol: 0 Mg   PRO: 0 Gm
SF: 0 Gm   CHO: 11 Gm
Sodium: 0 Mg   Fat: 1 Gm

BAKED APPLE

1 medium apple
1/2 package sugar substitute
Cinnamon and nutmeg, to taste
1 tablespoon diet margarine

Core apple and place in shallow baking dish. Place cinnamon, nutmeg, and diet margarine in core of apple. Add 1/8 cup water to dish and cover tightly with plastic wrap. Bake in microwave 8 to 10 minutes.

Yield: 1 serving

Calories: 1 2 3
Exchanges: 2 Fruit
                  2 Fat

Cholesterol: 0   PRO: 0
SF: less than 1 Gm   CHO: 24 Gm
Sodium: 49 Mg   Fat: 3 Gm

BERRIES AND CREAM

2 pkgs. (3 oz.) nutrasweet Jello brand gelatin, strawberry flavor
2 cups boiling water
1 quart diet vanilla ice cream, softened
1/2 angel food cake, sliced in 12 strips
1 pint fresh strawberries
8 oz. non-dairy whipped topping

Dissolve gelatin in boiling water. Add ice cream by spoonsful, stirring until ice cream is completely melted. Meanwhile, trim off ends of angel food cake and place, cut ends down, around sides of an 8-inch springform pan. Spoon gelatin mixture into pan and chill until firm, at least 3 hours. Remove sides of pan. Garnish with fresh strawberries and non-dairy whipped topping.

Yield: 12 slices

Calories: 142 per slice
Exchanges: 1 Bread
             1 Fruit
             1/2 Fat

Cholesterol: 35 Mg   PRO: 8 Gm
S.F: 5 Gm   CHO: 23 Gm
Sodium: 138 Mg   Fat: 2 Gm

FLAMING FRUIT DESSERT

1 (16 oz.) can unsweetened peaches, undrained
1 cup seedless green grapes, halved
1 cup seedless red grapes, halved
1/4 cup unsweetened white grape juice
1/2 teaspoon grated orange rind
1/4 teaspoon ground cinnamon
1/4 teaspoon ground nutmeg
1/4 cup rum
3 cups vanilla ice milk

Combine first 7 ingredients in a medium skillet. Bring to a boil, cover, reduce heat and simmer just until fruit is thoroughly heated. Place rum in a small, long-handled pan, heat just until warm. Do not boil. Ignite rum with a long match and pour over fruit. Serve sauce over 1/2-cup portions of ice milk.

Yield: 6 servings.

Calories: 210 per serving
Exchanges: 1 Bread
             2 Fruit
             1 Fat

Cholesterol: 28 Mg   PRO: 3 Gm
SF: 1 Gm   CHO: 36 Gm
Sodium: 84 Mg   Fat: 6 Gm

GLAZED FRUIT TART

1 cup graham cracker crumbs
3 tablespoons diet margarine, melted
2 cups plain nonfat yogurt
5 tablespoons sugar
2 tablespoons all-purpose flour
1 egg
1 egg white
1/2 teaspoon almond extract
1 banana
2 kiwi
1 cup strawberries
3 tablespoons sieved sugar-reduced orange marmalade

Combine crumbs and margarine. Press on bottom and sides of 10-inch pie plate or tart pan. Bake in 350-degree oven for 5 minutes. While crust bakes, combine yogurt, sugar, flour, egg, egg white, and extract in bowl; blend well. Pour into crust. Return to oven and bake for 20 minutes or until set. Remove and cool. Arrange fruits, overlapping on yogurt. Brush with sieved marmalade. Refrigerate until ready to serve.

Yield: 8 servings

Calories: 217 per serving
Exchanges: 2 Bread
                 1 Fruit
                 1 Fat

Cholesterol: 37 Mg   PRO: 5 Gm
SF: 1 Gm   CHO: 38 Gm
Sodium: 135 Mg   Fat: 5 Gm

HOMEMADE ICE CREAM

5 eggbeaters or 10 egg whites
2 cups sugar
2 tablespoons vanilla extract
3 (13 oz.) cans skimmed evaporated milk
2 quarts 2% milk

Mix all ingredients together, chill several hours before starting. Freeze in an electric ice cream freezer. It takes approximately 25 minutes. The ice cream will have a delicious and very firm flavor if left to stand in freezer after hardened. Pack freezer with ice and salt for one hour.

Yield: 1 gallon

Calories: 108 per 1/2 cup serving
Exchanges: 1/2 milk
                1 1/2 Fruit

Cholesterol: 16 Mg		PRO: 7 Gm
SF: less than 1 Gm		CHO: 20 Gm
Sodium: 66 Mg		Fat: less than 1 Gm

ORANGE MOLDED DESSERT

2 envelopes unflavored gelatin
2 1/4 cups water, divided
1 (12 oz.) can frozen orange juice concentrate, undiluted
1 pint orange sherbet, softened
2 medium oranges, peeled, sectioned, and seeded
12 whole strawberries or orange twists (optional)
Vegetable cooking spray

Soften gelatin in 1/4 cup water in a mixing bowl, let stand 5 minutes.

Bring remaining 2 cups water to a boil, add gelatin, stirring until dissolved. Add orange juice concentrate, stir until melted. Fold in sherbet, chill until the consistency of unbeaten egg white. Fold orange sections into gelatin mixture, pour into 12 individual molds coated with cooking spray. Chill until firm, unmold onto serving dishes. Garnish with whole strawberries or orange twists, if desired.

Yield: 12 servings

Calories: 76 per serving
Exchanges: 2 Fruit

Cholesterol: 5 Mg   PRO: less than 1 Gm
SF: less than 1 Gm   CHO: 19 Gm
Sodium: 18 Mg   Fat: less than 1 Gm

PEACH-BLUEBERRY COBBLER

1/3 cup sugar
1 tablespoon corn starch
3/4 cup orange juice
1 1/2 cups fresh or frozen peach slices
1 cup fresh or frozen blueberries
1/2 cup all-purpose flour
1/2 cup whole wheat flour
1 1/2 teaspoons baking powder
1/3 cups skim milk
3 tablespoons vegetable oil
1 teaspoon sugar

In a small saucepan, stir together 1/3 cup sugar and corn starch; add orange juice. Cook and stir until bubbly. Add peaches and blueberries; cook until it is hot. Keep warm. Stir together flours and baking powder. Add milk and oil; stir until mixture forms a ball. On floured surface, pat into an 8-inch circle. Cut into 8 wedges. Spoon hot berry mixture into a 9- inch pie plate; immediately top with wedges. Sprinkle with 1 teaspoon sugar. Bake in 425-degree oven 25 to 30 minutes or until wedges are brown. Serve warm.

Yield: 8 servings

Calories: 164 per serving
Exchanges: 1 Bread
             1 Fruit
             1 Fat

Cholesterol: less than 1 Mg   PRO: 2 Gm
SF: less than 1 Gm   CHO: 30 Gm
Sodium: 62 Mg   Fat: 4 Gm

PEACH PARFAIT

1 package (4-serving) nutrasweet Jello brand gelatin,
    peach flavor
3/4 cup boiling water
1/2 cup cold water
Ice cubes
1 cup chopped or sliced peaches
1 cup thawed non-dairy topping

Completely dissolve gelatin in boiling water. Combine cold water and ice cubes to make 1 1/4 cups. Add to gelatin and stir until slightly thickened; remove any unmelted ice. Measure 3/4 cup and add peaches. Pour into 6 individual parfait glasses. Blend whipped topping into remaining gelatin and spoon into glasses. Chill until set, about 1 hour.

Yield: 6 servings

Calories: 51 per serving
Exchanges: 1/2 Fruit
           1/2 Fat

Cholesterol: 0 Mg   PRO: 0 Gm
SF: 3 Gm   CHO: 6 Gm
Sodium: 11 Mg   Fat: 3 Gm

STRAWBERRY SORBET

*1 pint fresh strawberries
3/4 cup orange juice
1/2 cup milk
1/4 cup honey
2 egg whites
1 tablespoon honey

Remove stems from berries. In a blender container, place berries, orange juice, milk, and 1/4 cup honey. Cover; blend 1 minute or until smooth. Put mixture into 9 X 9 X 2-inch pan. Cover, freeze 2 to 3 hours or until almost firm.

In a small mixer bowl, beat egg whites with electric mixer on medium speed until soft peaks form. Gradually add 1 tablespoon honey, beating on high speed until stiff peaks form. Break frozen mixture into chunks; transfer to chilled large mixer bowl. Beat with electric mixer until smooth. Fold in egg whites. Return to pan. To serve, scrape across frozen mixture with spoon and mound in dessert dishes.

Yield: 6 servings

Calories: 84 per serving
Exchanges: 2 Fruit

Cholesterol: 0 Mg	PRO: 2 Gm
SF: less than 1 Gm	CHO: 19 Gm
Sodium: 30 Mg	Fat: 0 Gm

*May substitute 2 cups fresh ripe peaches.

Southern Traditions

HOLIDAY DINNER

Sliced Ham
Turkey Breast
Cornbread Dressing/Giblet Gravy
Green Peas
Candied Yams
Roll/Margarine
Cranberry sauce
Ambrosia Salad
Pecan Pie

Calories: 1,843

Cholesterol: 144 Mg   PRO: 42 Gm
SF: 7 Gm   CHO: 205 Gm
Sodium: 2,063 Mg   Fat: 95 Gm

SOUTHERN DINNER

Southern Fried Chicken
Mashed   Potatoes/Gravy
Corn on the Cob
Butterbeans
Roll/Margarine
Congealed Salad
Chocolate Cake

Calories: 1,435

Cholesterol: 273 Mg   PRO: 87 Gm
SF: 16 Gm   CHO: 143 Gm
Sodium: 1863 Mg   Fat: 59 Gm

OLD-FASHIONED TEA CAKES

1 cup margarine
1 1/2 cups sugar
2 eggs
1 teaspoon vanilla
Dash salt
1 teaspoon soda dissolved in hot water
3 cups flour
1/2 teaspoon baking powder

Cream margarine and sugar. Add remaining ingredients to this mixture. Roll 1/4" thick and cut with a cookie cutter. Bake at 350 degrees for 18-20 minutes until slightly browned.

Yield: 2 dozen

Calories: 136 per cookie

*Exchanges: Not acceptable for diabetics.

Cholesterol: 23 Mg   PRO: 2 Gm
SF: less than 1 Gm   CHO: 23 Gm
Sodium: 147 Mg   Fat: 4 Gm

AUNT ERA'S JAM CAKE

2 cups sugar
1 cup butter
1 cup buttermilk
1 cup nuts
1 cup dates or raisins
1 teaspoon soda

1 cup shortening
3 eggs
1 cup blackberry jam
3 cups all-purpose flour
1 cup coconut

Cream shortening, butter, and sugar. Add eggs. Mix flour and soda together and add to above mixture alternately with buttermilk, beginning and ending with flour mixture. Add remaining ingredients. Pour into three layer pans which are lined with waxed paper. Bake at 325 degrees until done.

FILLING:

2 cups sugar
2 tablespoons all-purpose flour
1 1/2 cups milk
1 cup butter

Cook until thick. Remove from heat and add 1 cup nuts, 1 cup raisins, and 1 cup coconut.

Yield: 12 slices

Calories: 1,024 per slice

*Exchanges: Not acceptable for diabetics.

Cholesterol: 155 Mg   PRO: 11 Gm
SF: 24 Gm   CHO: 119 Gm
Sodium: 436 Mg   Fat: 56 Gm

CARROT CAKE

1 1/2 cups vegetable oil	1 teaspoon salt
2 cups sugar	2 teaspoons soda
*4 eggs or 1 cup Eggbeaters	3 cups grated carrot
2 cups all-purpose flour	1/2 teaspoon vanilla extract
2 teaspoons baking powder	1 cup chopped pecans
2 teaspoons ground cinnamon	

Cream oil and sugar in a large bowl. Add eggs one at a time, beating well after each addition. Stir in dry ingredients; stir in carrots. Add flour mixture, vanilla, and nuts to creamed mixture. Pour batter in 3 cake pans or one 9 X 13-inch pan. Bake 375 degrees for 45 minutes to 1 hour.

ICING:

3/4 cup margarine
1- 8 oz. cream cheese
1-16 oz. box powdered sugar

Beat ingredients well, spread over cake.

9 X 13-inch Pan	9-inch Pan
Yield: 16 slices	Yield: 12 slices
Calories: 489 per slice	Calories: 624 per slice

*Exchanges: Not acceptable for diabetics.

Cholesterol: 84 Mg	Cholesterol: 112 Mg
SF: 7 Gm	SF: 9 Gm
Sodium: 390 Mg	Sodium: 520 Mg
PRO: 5 Gm	PRO: 6 Gm
CHO: 43 Gm	CHO: 60 Gm
Fat: 33 Gm	Fat: 40 Gm

* This recipe was calculated using real eggs.

CHOCOLATE CAKE

1 cup cocoa
2 cups boiling water
1 cup margarine, softened
2 1/2 cups sugar
4 eggs
1 teaspoon vanilla extract
2 3/4 cups all-purpose flour
2 teaspoons baking soda
1/2 teaspooon baking powder
1/2 teaspoon salt

Combine cocoa and boiling water.   Stir until smooth and set aside.
Combine sugar, margarine, eggs, and vanilla.   Beat with mixer 5
minutes until light and fluffy.   Combine   dry ingredients, adding
sugar slowly to cocoa mixture, beating with mixer on low speed.   Do
not OVERBEAT.   Pour batter into 3 pans sprayed with nonstick spray.
Bake at 350 degrees for 25 to 30 minutes.   Cool in pans 10 minutes.
Remove from pans and cool on cake racks.

FROSTING:

3/4 cup cocoa   1 cup confectioners sugar
1/3 cup milk   10 tablespoons margarine (softened)

Cream margarine in mixing bowl.   Add cocoa and confectioners sugar,
alternating with milk.   Blend in vanilla. Add additional milk for
desired consistency.   Garnish with chocolate curls or pecans.

Yield: 12   slices

Calories: 1,027   per   slice

*Exchanges: Not acceptable for diabetics.

Cholesterol: 98 Mg   PRO: 8 Gm
SF: 3 Gm   CHO: 107 Gm
Sodium: 127 Mg   Fat: 63 Gm

FRANCIS BAYS' FRENCH LEMON PIE

Mama Bays' pie crust*
1 cup sugar
1/4 cup all-purpose flour
4 eggs
1 cup corn syrup
4 tablespoons margarine, melted
Juice of one lemon
Grated lemon rind

Beat eggs until yellow. Add syrup, margarine, lemon juice, and rind.
Blend flour and sugar. Add to egg mixture. Pour into unbaked pie
shell. Bake 45 minutes in a 400 degree oven.

This recipe dates back to the late 1800's. Of course, butter
was used instead of margarine.

Yield: 8 slices

Calories: 437 per slice

*Exchanges: Not acceptable for diabetics.

Cholesterol: 137 Mg	PRO:	5 Gm
SF: 2 Gm	CHO:	75 Gm
Sodium: 120 Mg	Fat:	13 Gm

* See Page 211 for Mama Bays' Pie Crust.

HILL WOMAN'S SPECIAL FRUIT CAKE
(This recipe is over a hundred years old)

1 cup white sherry
2 sticks of butter plus 2 tablespoons
2 cups sugar
3/4 teaspoon lemon extract
1 teaspoon vanilla extract
2 quarts pecans
1 lb. white raisins
1 lb. candied pineapple
2 lbs. candied red cherries
1 lb. green candied cherries
4 cups flour (Reserve one cup for fruit and nuts)
1/2 teaspoon salt
5 eggs

Mix 1 cup flour with fruit and nuts. Cream butter and sugar. Add 1 egg at a time, beating well after each one that has been added. Add food extracts, salt, and 3 cups of flour. Fold fruit and nut mixture into cake batter. To prepare pans, cut brown paper to fit pans. Generously spray with cooking spray and dust with flour. Makes: 2-tube pans and 2 loaf pans. Bake in 250-degree oven 3 hours for tube pans and 1 1/2 hours for loaf pans. Five minutes before taking cakes from oven; pour 1 cup of sherry over tube pan and 1/4 -1/2 cup over loaf pans. Allow to bubble into cakes 5 minutes in the oven. Cool approximately 15 minutes. Peel brown paper from cakes. Cakes taste best when cured about 1 month before the holidays.

Yield: 56 slices

Calories: 391 per slice

*Exchanges: Not acceptable for diabetics.

Cholesterol: 35 Mg   PRO: 28 Gm
SF: 3 Gm   CHO: 36 Gm
Sodium: 85 Mg   Fat: 15 Gm

NEW YORK STYLE CHEESECAKE

FILLING:

6 eggs
2 1/2 tablespoons flour
5 (8 oz.) cream cheese

1/4 cup milk
1 3/4 cups sugar
2-3 squirts lemon

Cream the cheese and sugar at low speed. When blended, add eggs, flour, milk, and lemon juice. Press remaining dough to sides of pan. Pour in filling. Cook 12 minutes in preheated 475-degree oven, then turn down to 300 degrees for 35 minutes. Turn oven off and allow cake to stay in hot oven for 30 minutes. Allow to cool completely. If cheesecake cracks while baking, that's okay.

CRUST:

3/4 cup margarine
1/4 cup sugar
1 1/4 cups flour
1 egg yolk

Mix and form dough. Chill in the refrigerator 1 hour. Press dough into the bottom of a 10-inch springform pan. Cook 8 minutes in a preheated oven 400 degrees.

Yields: 12 servings

Calories: 668 per serving

*Exchanges: Not acceptable for diabetics.

Cholesterol: 287 Mg   PRO: 12 Gm
SF: 23 Gm   CHO: 47 Gm
Sodium: 23 Mg   Fat: 48 Gm

AUNT RUTH'S PEACH PIE

Mama Bays' pie shell
3 peaches (fresh)
3 eggs
1 cup sugar
2 tablespoons flour
1/2 stick margarine

Line unbaked pie crust with thinly sliced peaches. Blend eggs, flour, sugar, and melted margarine together. Pour over peaches. Bake at 350 degrees for 30-40 minutes or until set.

Yield: 8 servings

Calories: 224 per serving with crust

*Exchanges: Not acceptable for diabetics.

Cholesterol: 102 Mg	PRO:	8 Gm
SF: 3 Gm	CHO:	30 Gm
Sodium: 93 Mg	Fat:	8 Gm

* See page 211 for Mama Bays' Pie Crust.

GRANDMOTHER WARD'S EGG CUSTARD PIE

5 eggs
1 3/4 cups milk
1 cup sugar
3/4 stick margarine
1 teaspoon vanilla

Heat milk, sugar, margarine, and vanilla until margarine melts. Beat egg whites, then fold egg yolks into egg white. Pour milk mixture over egg mixture and blend. Pour into uncooked crust and bake at 350 degrees for 25 to 30 minutes.

Yield: 8 slices

Calories: 334 per slice

*Exchanges: Not acceptable for diabetics.

Cholesterol: 178 Mg   PRO: 8 Gm
SF: 9 Gm   CHO: 44 Gm
Sodium: 472 Mg   Fat: 14 Gm

*Calories were calculated using Mama Bays' Pie Crust on page 211.

GRANNY HARRELL'S COCONUT PIE

1 cup coconut
1 cup sugar
1 1/2 tablespoons margarine
1/4 teaspoon salt
2 cups scalded milk
3 tablespoons corn starch
2 egg yolks, large

Cook all ingredients except coconut together until thickened. Add coconut and stir. Cool and pour into pie shell.

MERINGUE

2 egg whites
6 teaspoons sugar
Vanilla to taste

Beat until egg whites are stiff, gradually adding sugar. Pour meringue over pie filling and bake in 350-degree oven until browned. Sprinkle with coconut.

Yield: 8 slices

Calories: 374 per 1/8 pie

*Exchanges: Not acceptable for diabetics.

Cholesterol: 131 Mg   PRO: 7 Gm
SF: 7 Gm   CHO: 55 Gm
Sodium: 439 Mg   Fat: 14 Gm

*Caloires were calculated using Mama Bays' Pie Crust on page 211.

MAMA BAYS' PIE CRUST

3 cups all-purpose flour
2 sticks margarine
1/2 teaspoon salt
1/2 cup ice-cold water
1 tablespoon vinegar

Mix flour and salt. Cut in cold margarine with fork until well blended. Add water and vinegar; work into a ball. Chill one hour before rolling out and placing into a pie pan. Bake 350 degrees until brown.

Yields: 16 servings=2 pie crusts

Calories: 98 per serving
Exchanges: 1 Bread
            1 Fat

Cholesterol: 0 Mg   PRO: 2 Gm
SF: 1 Gm   CHO: 18 Gm
Sodium: 130 Mg   Fat: 2 Gm

SOUTHERN PECAN PIE

#1		#2
1 cup sugar		1 cup sugar
1 cup corn syrup light or dark	OR	1 cup corn syrup light or dark
1 stick butter		1 stick margarine
3 eggs		3/4 cup eggbeaters
1 cup pecans		1 cup pecans

Put sugar into bowl. Add one egg at a time to sugar, beating until well mixed. Stir in syrup, melted margarine, and pecans. When well blended, pour into unbaked pie shell. Bake at 400 degrees 40-45 minutes.

Yields: 8 Servings

#1
Calories: 442 per serving

#2
Calories: 424 per serving

*Exchanges: Not acceptable for diabetics.

Cholesterol: 133 Mg
SF: 8 Gm
Sodium: 174 Mg
PRO: 4 Gm
CHO: 57 Gm
Fat: 22 Gm

Cholesterol: 0 Mg
SF: 2 Gm
Sodium: 163 Mg
PRO   4 Gm
CHO: 57 Gm
Fat: 20 Gm

*Calculations were made using Mama Bays' Pie Crust.   See Page 211.

SWEET POTATO PIE

1 cup cooked sweet potatoes, mashed
1 teaspoon vanilla
1/2 stick diet margarine
1 cup sugar
1 egg or 1/4 cup egg substitute
Dash of salt
Dash cinnamon and nutmeg

Mix ingredients together. Pour into crust* and bake 10 minutes in 400-degree oven and then in 350-degree oven until done.

Yield: 8 slices

Calories: 154 per slice without crust

*Exchanges: Not acceptable for diabetics.

Cholesterol:	0 Mg	PRO:	4 Gm
SF: 2 Gm		CHO:	50 Gm
Sodium:	207 Mg	Fat:	2 Gm

* See Page 211 for Mama Bays' Pie Crust.

4 LAYER DELIGHT

FIRST LAYER: 1 cup all-purpose flour
1 stick margarine
1 cup pecans

Mix and press into 13 X 9-inch pan. Bake 350 degrees 20-25 minutes. Cool.

SECOND LAYER: 8 oz. cream cheese
1 cup confectioners sugar
3/4 cup Cool Whip or non-dairy topping

Blend cheese and sugar. Fold in non-dairy topping. Spread on first layer.

THIRD LAYER: 1 package vanilla instant pudding
1 package chocolate instant pudding
3 cups milk

Blend. When it beings to thicken, pour over second layer.

FOURTH LAYER: 1 1/4 cups Cool Whip
1/4 cup pecans

Spread with non-dairy topping and sprinkle with nuts.

Yield: 16 servings

Calories: 500 per serving

*Exchanges: Not acceptable for diabetics.

Cholesterol: 22 Mg   PRO: 48 Gm
SF: 11 Gm   CHO: 32 Gm
Sodium: 254 Mg   Fat: 20 Gm

Just For Kids

EASY SLOPPY JOES

2 1/2 lbs. ground turkey
2 cups chopped onion
1 can tomato paste (6-oz. can)
1/2 cup catsup
1/4 cup tomato juice
2 tablespoons worcestershire sauce
2 tablespoons prepared mustard
2 tablespoons lemon juice
1 teaspoon salt
1/4 teaspoon pepper
6 hamburger buns, split and toasted

Combine ground turkey and onion in a large skillet; cook until meat is browned and onion is tender. Pour mixture into a colander, and pat dry with a paper towel. Wipe pan drippings from skillet with a paper towel. Return meat mixture to skillet and add remaining ingredients except buns. Simmer 15 to 20 minutes, stirring frequently. To serve, spoon 1/2 cup meat mixture over each bun half.

Yields: 12 servings

Calories: 253 per serving
Exchanges: 3 Meat
            1 Bread
            1 Vegetable

Cholesterol: 71 Mg   PRO: 25 Gm
SF: 2 Gm   CHO: 18 Gm
Sodium: 451 Mg   Fat: 9 Gm

SOFT CHICKEN TACOS

1 package (12) flour tortillas-6 inch
4 (4 oz.) chicken breasts, skinned
1 package taco seasoning mix
6 oz. low-fat cheddar cheese, shredded
12 tablespoons sour cream (optional)
Shredded lettuce
Chopped tomato
Chopped onion

Simmer chicken in water until done. Cut meat into small pieces. In a skillet, combine cooked chicken, taco seasoning, and 1 1/2 cups water. Bring to a boil, then simmer to desired consistency (10-15 minutes). Heat tortillas in microwave or iron skillet. Place 2 oz. chicken mix in the center of each tortilla. Top with 1/2 oz. cheese, 1 tablespoon sour cream, shredded lettuce, chopped tomato, and chopped onion. Roll up.

Yield: 12 tacos

Calories: 231 per taco
Exchange: 2 Meat
             1 Bread
             1 Fat

Cholesterol: 57 Mg   PRO: 15 Gm
SF: 5 Gm   CHO: 18 Gm
Sodium: 173 Mg   Fat: 11 Gm

TASTY TACO PIE

1 pound ground turkey
2 (8 oz.) cans tomato sauce
1 taco seasoning mix (1.25 oz. pkg.)
1 (8-oz. can) refrigerated quick crescent dinner rolls
6 slices liteline cheese, chopped
1 cup shredded lettuce
1/2 cup chopped tomato
1/4 cup jalapeno peppers, sliced (optional)

Brown meat, drain. Stir in tomato sauce and seasoning mix, simmer
5 minutes. Press dough onto bottom and sides of ungreased 12-inch
pizza pan, pressing edges together to form seal. Prick bottom and
sides with fork. Bake at 375 degrees for 10-12 minutes or until deep
golden brown. Fill with meat mixture, cover with chopped liteline
cheese. Continue baking until cheese begins to melt. Top with
remaining ingredients.

Yields: 6 servings

Calories: 240 per serving
Exchanges: 2 1/2 Meat
              1 Bread
              1/2 Vegetable
              1 Fat

Cholesterol: 72 Mg   PRO: 10 Gm
SF: 3 Gm   CHO: 18 Gm
Sodium: 80 Mg   Fat: 14 Gm

TOSTADA

2 flour tortillas (6-inch diameter)
1/2 cup mashed pinto or red kidney beans
1/4 teaspoon chili powder
1 cup shredded chicken or cooked ground turkey
1 slice liteline cheese, chopped
1/2 cup shredded lettuce
6 tomato slices
4 tablespoons each: chopped onion
                      bell pepper
                      bottled salsa

Wrap tortillas in foil; heat in 350-degree oven for 5 minutes. Set aside. In small bowl, season beans with chili powder. Spread over warmed tortilla. Top with chicken and cheese. Broil 3 inches from heat to melt cheese. Top with lettuce and tomato. Serve with onion, bell pepper, and salsa.

Yield: 2 servings

Calories: 213 per serving
Exchanges: 1 Meat
            1 Bread
            1 Vegetable

Cholesterol: 41 Mg   PRO: 14 Gm
SF: 2 Gm   CHO: 28 Gm
Sodium: 350 Mg   Fat: 5 Gm

VEGETABLE PIZZA WITH OAT BRAN CRUST

Vegetable cooking spray
2 teaspoons vegetable oil
7 cups thinly sliced or chopped vegetables:
Yellow squash, mushrooms, bell pepper, onions, and
   broccoli flowerettes
1 (8 oz.) can no-salt-added tomato sauce
1 (6 oz.) can no-salt-added tomato paste
2 tablespoons red wine vinegar
1/2 teaspoon dried whole oregano
1 clove garlic, minced
3/4 cup (3 oz.) finely shredded part-skim mozzarella
   cheese
3/4 cup (3 oz.) finely shredded 40% less-fat cheddar cheese
*Pizza crust

Coat a large nonstick skillet with vegetable cooking spray; add oil. Place over medium high heat until hot. Add vegetables and saute' until crisp-tender. Drain and set aside. Combine tomato sauce and next 5 ingredients in a medium saucepan. Bring to a boil, stirring constantly. Reduce heat and simmer, uncovered, 15 to 20 mintues or until thickened. Set aside. *Spread tomato sauce mixture evenly over pizza crust. Arrange vegetable mixture evenly over sauce. Combine mozzarella cheese and cheddar cheese and sprinkle evenly over top of pizza. Bake at 350 degrees for 30 minutes or until crust is golden brown and cheese melts.

Yields: 1 pizza (8 servings)

Calories: 119 per serving
Exchanges: 1 Meat
                   2 Vegetable

Cholesterol: 15 Mg   PRO: 7 Gm
SF: 3 Gm   CHO: 16 Gm
Sodium: 106 Mg   Fat: 3 Gm

*See Page 176 for pizza crust.

ORANGE JULIUS

1 cup 2% milk
6 oz. orange juice frozen concentrate
1 cup ice
1 cup water
1 teaspoon vanilla

Blend in blender.

Yield: 4 servings

Calories: 73
Exchanges: 1 Fruit

Cholesterol: 5 Mg   PRO: 2 Gm
SF: less than 1 Gm   CHO: 14 Gm
Sodium: 5 Mg   Fat: 1 Gm

MICROWAVE POPCORN

1. Pour 1/2 cup popcorn in the base . You need not add oil. Do not overload. Set cover on base.

2. Place popper in microwave oven and cook on HIGH (100%) for 3 to 5 minutes.

3. Grasp handles of both base and cover to remove the popper from the microwave. (Use potholders or oven mitts.)

4. Pour popcorn into pan. Spray generously with butter flavored Pam and sprinkle with popcorn seasoning.

Yield: 3 cups - 1 serving

Calories: 84 per serving
Exchanges: 1 Bread

Cholesterol: 0 Mg   PRO: 3 Gm
SF: 0 Gm   CHO: 18 Gm
Sodium: 300 Mg   Fat: less than 1 Gm

CHEWY OATMEAL COOKIES

2 sticks margarine
1/2 cup brown sugar
1/2 cup white sugar
1/4 cup Eggbeaters
1 teaspoon vanilla
1 cup all-purpose flour
5 cups oatmeal
1/2 teaspoon salt
1/2 teaspoon soda
Cinnamon

Preheat oven to 350 degrees. Beat together, margarine, sugar, egg substitute, and vanilla until creamy. Blend all dry ingredients and add to creamed mixture. Drop by rounded teaspoons onto cookie sheet that has been sprayed with nonstick cooking spray. Bake 8-10 minutes. Let set on cookie sheet a few minutes before removing.

Yield: 6 dozen

Calories: 63 per cookie

*Exchanges: Not acceptable for diabetics.

Cholesterol: 0 Mg   PRO: 1 Gm
SF: less than 1 Gm   CHO: 8 Gm
Sodium: 51 Mg   Fat: 3 Gm

CHOCOLATE MILLIONAIRES

1/3 cup powdered milk
4 packages Equal
2 teaspoons cocoa
2 1/2 tablespoons water-more or less
1/2 teaspoon vanilla or butternut flavoring
3/4 oz. dry oatmeal (1/3 cup)
1 tablespoon crunchy peanut butter

Mix all ingredients together. Roll into 12 individual balls.

Yield: 12 pieces

Calories: 37 per piece
Exchanges: 1/2 Bread

Cholesterol: less than 1 Mg   PRO: 1 Gm
SF: less than 1 Gm   CHO: 6 Gm
Sodium: 39 Mg   Fat: 1 Gm

CHOCOLATE YOGURT

8 oz. low-fat yogurt
1 package chocolate milk maker with nutrasweet
   (Swiss Miss)
Strawberry milk maker may be substituted.
1 package Equal or sugar substitute (optional)

Mix and chill.

Yield: 1 serving

Calories: 121
Exchange: 1 Milk

Cholesterol: 14 Mg   PRO: 12 Gm
SF: less than 1 Gm   CHO: 16 Gm
Sodium: 159 Mg   Fat: 1 Gm

OAT & DATE COOKIES

3/4 cup margarine
3/4 cup brown sugar
1/4 cup Eggbeaters
1/2 cup sour cream
1 teaspoon vanilla flavoring
1 1/2 cups flour
1/2 teaspoon baking soda
1/2 teaspoon salt
1 cup oats
1 cup chopped dates
1/2 cup chopped nuts

Cream sugar and margarine. Add next three ingredients and beat. Combine dry ingredients. Add to creamed mixture. Add remaining ingredients. Drop by spoonful onto ungreased cookie sheet. Bake 375 degrees for 10 minutes until browned.

Yield: 3 dozen (36 cookies)

Calories: 92 per cookie

*Exchanges: Not acceptable for diabetics.

Cholesterol: 9 Mg   PRO: 1 Gm
SF: less than 1 Gm   CHO: 13 Gm
Sodium: 87 Mg   Fat: 4 Gm

OATMEAL COOKIES

Crisp version of the old favorite.

1/2 cup margarine
3/4 cup brown sugar
1 egg
1 teaspoon vanilla
1/2 teaspoon soda

1/2 teaspoon salt
3/4 teaspoon cinnamon
1 1/4 cups rolled oats
3/4 cup whole wheat flour

Cream margarine, sugar, egg, and vanilla. Sift together flour, soda, salt, and cinnamon. Add to margarine mixture. Mix until smooth. Stir in rolled oats. Drop by teaspoon onto ungreased baking sheet. Bake at 375 degrees 10-12 minutes.

Yield: 48 cookies

Calories: 38 per cookie

*Exchanges: Not acceptable for diabetics.

Cholesterol: 5 Mg
SF: less than 1 Gm
Sodium: 153 Mg

PRO: less than 1 Gm
CHO: 6 Gm
Fat: 1 Gm

PEANUT BUTTER BALLS

1/4 cup peanut butter
1/4 cup powdered milk
1/4 cup raisins
4 graham crackers (2 X 2-inch square), broken in pieces
1 teaspoon vanilla
Dash cinnamon

Cream peanut butter with 2 tablespoons milk until well blended. Add remaining ingredients. Mix well. Drop on aluminum foil or wax paper in balls about 1 inch in diameter. Place in freezer until ready to serve.

Yield: 16 Balls

Calories: 68 per 2
Exchanges: 1/2 Bread
1 Fat

Cholesterol: less than 1 Mg PRO: 1 Gm
SF: less than 1 Gm CHO: 3 Gm
Sodium: 8 Mg Fat: 2 Gm

PEANUT BUTTER COOKIES

1/2 cup margarine
1 cup brown sugar
1 egg
1/2 cup peanut butter
1 teaspoon vanilla
1 1/4 cups whole wheat flour
1/2 teaspoon soda
1/4 teaspoon salt

Cream margarine, sugar, egg, peanut butter, and vanilla. Sift together flour, soda, and salt. Add to creamed mixture. Mix until smooth. Shape teaspoonful into balls and place 2 inches apart on ungreased cookie sheet. Flatten lightly with a fork. Bake at 375 degrees 10-12 minutes.

Yield: 48 cookies

Calories: 46 per cookie

*Exchanges: Not acceptable for diabetics.

Cholesterol: 5 Mg	PRO: 1 Gm
SF: less than 1 Gm	CHO: 6 Gm
Sodium: 5 Mg	Fat : 2 Gm

Nutritional Information

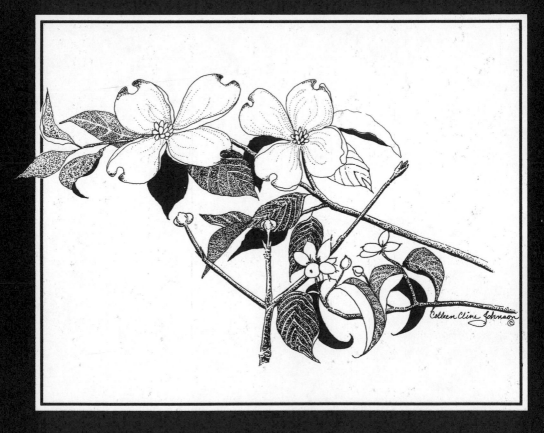

Colleen Cline Johnson

HOW TO SHOP AND READ LABELS

There is much confusing information concerning labels and how to read labels. We would like to help simplify the process to help you understand label reading and be prepared to make good nutritional choices. Let's look at the calories on a food label.

EXAMPLE: FOOD LABEL

Beef & Sauce Ingredients: tomatoes, beef broth, mushrooms, tomato paste, onion, red wine, starch, parmesan cheese, sugar, natural & artifical flavorings, chicken fat, hydrolyzed plant protein, salt, spices, vegetable oil, citric acid & garlic.
Spaghetti Ingredients: cooked spaghetti & vegetable oil.

NUTRITIONAL DATA:

SERVING SIZE.................................9.00 OZ
SERVINGS PER CONTAINER......................1
CALORIES..210
PROTEIN...13 GM
CARBOHYDRATE..............................26 GM
FAT...4 GM
SODIUM..770 MG
POTASSIUM.......................................550MG

PERCENTAGES OF U. S.
DAILY ALLOWANCES (U.S. RDA)

PROTEIN.........20	RIBOFLAVIN.....10
VITAMIN A...25	NIACIN..............10
VITAMIN C....20	CALCIUM.............8
THIAMINE.....10	IRON.....................*

*CONTAINS LESS THAN 2% OF THE U.S. RDA OF THIS NUTRIENT

Calories are listed per serving. Be sure to determine the number of servings provided per container. Many canned and frozen foods have two (2) or more servings per container. Not only must we look at more than just calories, but where they come from.

Food labels do not tell you how many calories come from fat. To find out, you must first look at the number of grams of fat on the label.

EXAMPLE

$$\frac{4 \text{ GMS FAT X 9 CALORIES PER GM=}}{210 \text{ CALORIES}} \quad \frac{36 \text{ Gms}}{210 \text{ Calories}} = 17\% \text{ Fat}$$

The product should not exceed more than 30% of its calories from fat. Also note the source of fat. In this case, chicken fat is a source of fat and considered a saturated fat, increasing cholesterol. Cutting back on fat can help you control your weight and lipid levels.

Depending on your caloric requirements, your fat allowance will vary. You must first determine the amount of calories to maintain ideal weight. No more than 30% of your calories should come from fat.

EXAMPLE

TOTAL CALORIES	CALORIES FROM FAT PER DAY	MAX GRAMS FAT PER DAY
1500	450 (1500 X 30%)	50 GMS (450/9)

CHOLESTEROL is not always listed on the label. When listed, it is in milligrams per serving or milligrams per 100 grams. Remember, your intake of cholesterol should not exceed 300 mg per day.

SODIUM is listed in milligrams. A safe and adequate intake is 3000-4000 milligrams per day (3-4 gms).

RDA'S are standards used in food labeling recommending proper amounts of vitamins and minerals to maintain health. For further analysis of your nutritional health, check with a registered licensed dietitian.

INGREDIENT LIST

Ingredients are listed in order of quantity. Beware of products which list fat or sugar as one of the first ingredients. Remember, fat can be listed in many ways: lard, butter, chicken fat, margarine, oil, or shortening.

DIETETIC FOODS

May not be low in calories. Many times sugar is removed from a product and extra salt or fat may be added. "Sugar Free", "Part Skim", "Non-Dairy", "Low Butterfat" or"Lite" does not necessarily mean a food is low-calorie or low-fat.

The following is a list of definitions that will enable you to make better food choices.

****

Extra lean: No more than 5% fat by weight not by calories.

Leaner: 25% or less fat by weight than the regular product.

Sugar free: Contains no table sugar (sucrose); however, may have fructose, corn syrup, honey, sorbital, or other sweeteners. Not always low in calories.

Sodium free: No more than 5 mg per serving.

Very low sodium: No more than 35 mg sodium per serving.

Low sodium: No more than 140 mg sodium per serving.

Reduced sodium: 25% less sodium than regular product.

No salt added/Salt free: No salt added in processing; however, could have natural sodium or sodium from other products added.

Low in calories: No more than 40 calories per serving.

****

SUPERMARKETING

Dairy Foods:

* Use low-fat yogurt instead of mayonnaise or sour cream in dishes.

* Part skim mozzarella, string cheese, low-fat ricotta and the many "lite" reduced calorie cheeses help us.

* Low-fat versions of milk, buttermilk, cottage cheese, and yogurts are good nutritional values.

Meats:

* Select lean cuts: round steak, flank steak, tenderloin, loin chops, ground round.

* Use the "select" or diet lean cuts.

* Limit meats high in saturated fats such as liver, bacon, ribs, sausage and duck. Venison is considered a lean meat.

Fresh Fish and Poultry:

* Buy skinless chicken or remove skin before cooking.
One-half of the calories in chicken are from the skin.

* Fish from deep waters are excellent sources of the omega-three (3) fatty acids which aid in lowering cholesterol levels. Examples are: salmon, sable fish, sea trout, bluefish, and mackerel. Catfish is a southern favorite much lower in saturated fat than beef and pork, supplying smaller amounts of omega-3 fatty acids.

* Most pre-breaded chicken and turkey are usually high in sodium and fat.

* Lean fresh ground turkey or chicken is an excellent substitute for ground beef.

Produce:

* Fresh vegetables are always a good choice. Be careful of added sodium.

* Remember, skins of fruits, vegetables, and seeds are good sources of fiber.

* Fruits and vegetables are good sources of vitamin A and C.

Breads/Cereals:

* Look for "whole wheat" or "whole grain" at the beginning of the label.

* Choose cereals with at least 2 grams of fiber per serving.

* Select cereals with less than 2 grams of fat per serving.

* Sugar in many cereals is extremely high. Do not exceed 8 grams per serving.

* Use enriched breads. The "lite" breads can help cut calories.

Fats:

* The softer the margarine the better.

* Use only margarine or oil with unsaturated fats. (Example: corn oil, safflower, and cottonseed.)

* Lite mayonnaise has about 1/2 the calories of regular.

* Use diet dressings to cut fat calories. May be used as a marinade for meats and poultry.

* Reduced calorie margarines can save calories.

Frozen Foods:

* Purchase frozen poultry and fish without breading to lower fat and sodium.

* Do not use frozen vegetables in sauces. Plain frozen is a good choice.

* Look for frozen dinners with less than 30% of the calories from fat and less than 800 mg of sodium.

* Frozen fruit juices are often less expensive than the prepared juice.

DELI:

* Sliced lean turkey, roast beef, and ham are good choices.

* Lean ham or canadian bacon are good choices to season southern vegetables to lower fat versus using bacon drippings and ham hocks.

* Turkey or chicken weiners are still high fat and high in sodium-limit their use.

* Processed lunch meats should be 95% fat free.

PACKAGED PRODUCTS:

* Read labels - palm, palm kernel, and coconut oil are high in saturated fats and should be avoided.

* Graham crackers, animal crackers, and gingersnaps have less fat and sugar than most other cookies.

* Microwave popcorn is usually high fat and/or high sodium.

* Thick unsalted pretzels are a better snack than most chips.

* Most prepackaged mixes are high in sodium.

PROTEIN

The general requirement for protein in the American diet is 0.8 g/kg body weight per day in the average man and woman.

(NOTE:) Disease states, lactation, pregnancy, and children's requirements are not accounted for in this formula. Check with a registered licensed dietitian or nutritionist for specifics in these areas.

EXAMPLE:

> If a woman weighed 130 pounds, what would her protein requirement be?
>
> 1st - Convert pounds to kilograms by dividing 130/2.2 = 59kg.
>
> 2nd - kg x 0.8g = grams/protein/day
> 59kg x 0.8g = 47 grams/protein/day required

The required amount of protein is usually no more than 10% of the total daily calories. Animal sources of protein also contain fat. It is good nutritional practice to include at least one-third of protein from complete proteins, although this is not a hard and fast rule. We recommend seeing a registered nutritionist in combining only incomplete proteins. Often the protein requirement is much higher.

COMPLETE PROTEINS	INCOMPLETE PROTEINS
Milk	Grains And Breads
Meat	Vegetables
Fish	Rice
Poultry	Potatoes
Eggs	Beans
Cheese	Peas
	Nuts
	Seeds

Most Americans are consuming far more protein than they need. 6-8 ounces of meat or half a chicken is considered a portion at most meals, when in reality 3-4 ounces would more than meet our requirements, and we would all be healthier for it. We recommend 15-20% of your calories should come from protein. Remember, this is combining animal and vegetable proteins. Protein is necessary but also dangerous in extremely high amounts.

Too much protein is linked with obesity, high cholesterol leading to heart disease and high uric acid levels leading to impaired kidney function. Too much protein, leading to obesity, also increases the loss of calcium from the bones, or thinning of the bones, known as osteporosis.

Protein is necessary to repair worn out body tissue, to build new tissue, to supply heat and energy, and to play a role in the resistance of the body to disease.

Protein is necessary for many metabolic functions and contributes to numerous body secretions and fluids. Only a small amount of protein is actually needed by the body. It is a myth that athletes need large quantities of protein. Muscle growth is not enhanced by increased protein intake and has only a minor role as an energy source. Research now recognizes athletes do not need extra protein but extra carbohydrates to be used as fuel by their muscles. Too much protein can actually impair athletic performance, because the kidneys must pull water from the muscles to excrete the bi-products of large amounts of protein.

CARBOHYDRATES

A diet high in complex carbohydrates is generally recommended for good health. Complex carbohydrates provide most of the energy needed to work and stay alive. Many individuals with excess weight often associate weight gain with carbohydrates. This is most often not the problem. A diet high in complex carbohydrates usually gives you a full feeling because it is higher in fiber. Also, remember, carbohydrate foods are low in cholesterol in their natural state. A high fiber, high carbohydrate diet, along with physical activity, has been shown to reduce cholesterol levels, prevent cancer, diverticulosis, constipation, and has enabled many people to avoid coronary bypass operations. Many vitamins, minerals, and other essential nutrients, such as protein, are provided by carbohydrate foods.

EXCELLENT FOOD SOURCES ARE:

Whole Grain Cereals
Whole Wheat Bread
Brown Rice
Beans And Potatoes
Fruit
Vegetables
Potatoes with Skin

Carbohydrates supply 4 calories per gram. 50-55% of our diet should be composed of carbohydrates. Carbohydrates provide a protein sparing action. If sufficient carbohydrates are not available, the body will convert protein to energy. Carbohydrates are necessary for normal fat metabolism, aids in maintenance of nerve tissue, and among many other functions, indigestible carbohydrates aid in normal elimination. Carbohydrates are the sole source of energy for the brain.

Simple sugars or simple carbohydrates are sugars such as glucose, galactose, and fructose. Fruits and juices are composed largely of simple sugars. These are valuable sources of vitamins and minerals. Foods such as sucrose or table syrup, candies, and cookies usually contain mostly refined sugars.

SOURCES OF REFINED SUGARS

Cane Sugar	Sweetened Soft Drinks
Brown Sugar	Syrup
Candy	Jams
Cookies	Honey

It has been conclusive in our clinic that when individuals reduce calories to lose weight, they are more successful by first eliminating refined sugars and replacing them with complex carbohydrates.

FAT

Fat serves as a source of energy in the body and transport of fat soluble vitamins A, D, E, and K. Too much fat in the diet can lead to coronary artery disease. A diet high in fat is also thought to predispose an individual to some types of cancer.

Statistically, heart disease is the leading cause of death in the U.S., outnumbering cancer and accidents combined. The amount of fat in our diet can be directly related to cardiovascular disease.

Let's look at the clinical types of fat for which the physician tests. Cholesterol in the blood stream is produced from cholesterol in the foods we eat and cholesterol made in the liver and intestine. The body is capable of producing all the cholesterol needed without consuming additional cholesterol at all. Lab values vary for different age groups; however, greater than 200 mg/dl is considered too high for total blood cholesterol.

Fats do not mix with water but are transported in the blood stream by lipoproteins (Lipo means fat). There are lipoproteins VLDL, LDL, and HDL. These together equal total cholesterol.

LIPOPROTEIN:

VLDL (Triglycerides) + Cholesterol + Protein

FUNCTIONS:

Produced in liver and released into blood stream. After meals, used to store excess fat and carbohydrates in the blood stream. Responsible for buildup of plaque in blood stream.

NORMAL VALUE:

Not measured directly-calculated from triglyceride level.

$$VLDL = Trig/5$$

TO DECREASE RISK FACTORS:

Restrict alcohol, restrict refined carbohydrates. Eliminate sweets. Exercise. Lose weight, eat less saturated fat.

LIPOPROTEIN:

LDL

FUNCTION:

After triglycerides are utilized with body energy (VLDL-Trig), you are left with LDL containing mostly cholesterol and protein which are circulated in the blood stream.

NORMAL VALUE:

Women:	*135-145*	*mg/dl*
Men:	*120-135*	*mg/dl*

TO DECREASE RISK FACTOR:

Eat less saturated fat, eat less cholesterol. Exercise. Lose weight, if overweight.

LIPOPROTEIN:

HDL (GOOD CHOLESTEROL)

FUNCTION:

Removes cholesterol from LDL to take it to liver, where it is transformed into bile leaving the body. Prevents cholesterol from accumulating in the blood stream. Protects against coronary heart disease.

NORMAL VALUE:

Women: 29-80   mg/dl
Men: 29-80   mg/dl

TO DECREASE RISK FACTOR:

Exercise, stop smoking, lose weight, if overweight.

When planning a low cholesterol, low saturated fat diet, it is always recommended a registered dietitian be consulted. A low-fat diet needs to be individualized. What is right for one person may not be right for another.

If cholesterol is found to be higher than 200 mg/dl, restrict cholesterol in meats, dairy products, cheese, meat drippings, and gravies. Saturated fats are said to affect cholesterol to a greater extent than the actual cholesterol in the diet. Saturated fats are found in higher concentrations in red meats.

For example, 3 ounces of chicken and 3 ounces of beef have:

	S.F.	CHOL.
CHICKEN	2.5 gm	80 mg
LEAN GROUND BEEF	5.5 gm	80 mg

Similar amounts of cholesterol, however, when looking at the saturated fat present, makes it evident the ground beef has almost 2 1/2 times more saturated fat. That is why, to a greater extent, red meats tend to elevate cholesterol levels. Another hidden source of saturated fat is found commercially as coconut oil, palm oil, or any hydrogenated fat, (even hydrogenated vegetable fats). For this reason, red meats are restricted when people are trying to lower cholesterol levels.

In the clinic, we recommend eating mostly chicken, turkey, and fish, but eating a variety of meats. However, when eating some red meats, always choose the leaner cuts and be sure to watch portion size. For example:

Roast: Rump or Eye of the Round
Pork: Pork Loins
Steak: Sirloin

It is recommended that an individual keep cholesterol in the diet around 250-300 mg total fat in the diet to 30% of calories and, of those calories, no more than 10% in saturated fats.

There are three types of fat in the diet to consider. Below is a chart describing these fats, their use, and their source.

Monounsaturated Fats: *Liquid at room temperature may even be effective in lowering cholesterol by maintaining a high HDL or "Good" cholesterol.*

OIL	USE
Avocado	*Dressings*
Canola	*Stir-frying*
Safflower	*Sauteing*
High Oleic	*Frying*
Sesame	*Baking*
Olive	*Dressings*
Peanut Oil	*Sauteing*
	Dressings
	Marinades
	Stir-Frying
	Frying

Polyunsaturated Fats: *Liquid at room temperatures. Lowers LDL or "Bad" cholesterol.*

OIL	USE
Corn	*Stir-Frying*
Safflower	*Frying*
Soybean	*Baking*
Sunflower	*Dressings*
	Marinades

Saturated Fats: *May increase your cholesterol more than cholesterol containing foods. Saturated fats do not necessarily contain cholesterol. Coconut, palm, and palm kernel oils are saturated fats. They are used for frying, baking, and commerical goods.*

We do highly recommend seeing a registered dietitian. There is so much information to consider, diets can become complicated. In most cases, however, a person finds more freedom than originally expected, which will allow longterm adherence to diet.

SODIUM

Sodium is the substance in salt that when used
excessively has been shown to produce high blood
pressure in some individuals. Sodium also holds
water in the body, causing discouraging weight gain
and bloating which can mask one's weight loss.

Only about 1/3 of salt comes from adding salt to
foods. The remainder comes from processed foods.
Gradually reduce the amount of salt used. Just by
eliminating processed foods, one can gain far more
control over salt. Many food additives contain
sodium. Examples are baking powder, baking soda,
and MSG (monosodium glutamate). Use herbs and
spices to replace salt and experience the natural
flavor of foods you've missed for years. (Refer to
the seasoning chart). If you prefer to use processed
foods, many food processors are introducing "no
added salt" products or "reduced salt" in products.
Try to use fresh meats, fruits, and vegetables as
much as possible. Become familiar with complex
carbohydrates naturally low in sodium. For
example, instant oatmeal and grits have more
sodium on the average, whereas, plain oatmeal and
grits have little sodium. Diet carbonated drinks with
nutrasweet blends are usually between 35-55 mg
sodium and considered low sodium. Remember,
many medications contain sodium. The Food and
Drug Administration has guidelines for sodium. Any
food making a sodium claim must show how many
milligrams per serving:

*Sodium Free-contains less than 5 mg per serving

*Very Low Sodium-contains 35 mg or less per serving

*Low Sodium-contains 140 mg or less per serving

*Reduced Sodium-reduced by 75% or more below a comparable product it replaces

| *Unsalted *No Salt Added *Without Added Salt | Must have no salt in processing |

The American Heart Association recommends a diet containing 3 to 4 gms of sodium (1 gram=1000 mg). Generally, most Americans consume an average of 8-10 grams per day.

HIGH SODIUM FOODS

FOOD	MG
*1 Dill Pickle	1200
*1 Frankfurter	600-800
*1 Bouillon Cube	960
*1 Tablespoon Soy Sauce	850
*1 Cup Canned Soup	800
*1/2 Cup Canned Vegetables	250-300

**SODIUM CONTENT MAY VARY AMONG BRANDS. READ LABELS.

SEASONINGS

HERBS & SPICES

Basil	Compliments recipes with tomatoes or tomato sauce.
Bay Leaf	Adds nicely to soups, stews, and marinades.
Celery Seed	Adds flavor to soups and stock.
Chives	Can be substituted for raw onion in any recipe.
Garlic	Excellent in southern vegetables, soups, meats, and tomato based recipes.
Mustard (dry)	Adds spice to sauces or over roast chicken.
Oregano	Good in tomato based dishes.
Paprika	Mild pepper, adds color to dishes.
Rosemary	Excellent seasoning for poultry.
Tarragon	Goes well with poultry dishes.
Thyme	Combines well with Bay leaves in soups.

Cinnamon	Important in dessert preparation.
Cumin	A staple spice in Mexican foods.
Chili Powder	Used for a highly spiced flavor (Remember many commercial chili powders are 40% salt and 20% additives. Look for pure ground chili powder.)
Peppercorns	Green, red, white, and black peppercorns are available on the market. Excellent added to almost any dish.
Marjoram	Used in tomato dishes, eggplant, zucchini, lima beans, and eggs. Add to meats for a flavor similar to oregano.

OTHER SEASONINGS

Tomato Salsa	Excellent for added zest to any dish
Vinegars	Balsamic, champagne, rice, malt, and red wine vinegar are just a few of the varieties available. Enhances salads, vegetables, and many cold meat dishes.
Liquid Smoke	Excellent to add a hickory flavor to meats and vegetables.
Lemon Juice	Fresh squeezed adds zest to salads and marinades.
Reduced Sodium Soy Sauce	Reduces sodium. Good in stir fries and marinades.
Hot Sauces	Adds a hot spiced flavor to soups, vegetables, and marinades.
Butter Substitutes	Enables one to enjoy a buttery flavor without the concentrated fat calories. Read labels to compare sodium content.
Lite Dressings (Italian & Catalina)	Excellent marinade for meats, fish, and poultry.

Gumbo File'	Good in soup and vegetable dishes as a thickening and spice.
Curry Powder	Use in sauces to baste fish and chicken, or in cheese dishes.
Fennel Seed	Sprinkle top of breads before baking. Excellent to season broiled fish.
Sesame Seed	Sprinkle on breads before baking. Sprinkle on noodles, vegetables, and fish.
Parsley	Use as a garnish or add to rice, pastas, soups, stews, vegetables, fish, poultry, salads, and dressing

**Fresh spices have a more pungent flavor than dried. To enhance the flavor of dried spices, crush with spice mallet before using.

FIBER

Fiber has steadily decreased in the American diet. Americans average about 20 gms of fiber per day. We love our meats, fats, sugars, and refined foods, most of which have little or no dietary fiber. The recommendation for fiber is approximately 35-40 gms per day. Gradually increase fiber by 1 gram per day. Sudden changes in diet can cause gas, bloating, and even diarrhea. Steadily increasing fiber to 35-40 grams per day can lower blood cholesterol and blood sugar levels. Statistics show a high fiber diet can aid in preventing colon cancer, breast cancer, and diverticulitis.

WHAT IS FIBER?

Crude Fiber is mainly lignin and cellulose. This is the material in food that remains after treatment with acid and alkali. Most food composition tables give values for crude fiber.

Dietary Fiber is the most significant substance for the digestive tract and contains not only lignin and cellulose but hemicellulose, gums, and pectins not normally digested. Remember, the most important thing is to get a mixture of all the fibers in one's diet.

Fiber is classified as soluble and insoluble.

SOLUBLE	INSOLUBLE
Oats	Whole Grain Wheat
Oat Bran	Corn
Barley	Rye
Legumes	Vegetables
Pectin (Fruits)	Fruits
Psyllium	

Soluble fiber dispenses into a gel form when placed in liquid. These fibers aid in lowering cholesterol and blood sugar levels. Insoluble fibers do not dispense in liquid and add bulk and fullness to the diet, promoting normal bowel movements.

When restricting calories, insoluble fibers give one a feeling of fullness. When water soluble fibers are present, cholesterol binds with the fibers and leaves the body through the stool rather than being reabsorbed after digestion; therefore, the total cholesterol is reduced by high fiber foods in combination with a low-fat diet.

TYPES OF FIBER

<u>PECTIN</u>: Increase bulk and slows gastric emptying time; used widely in making jelly.
<u>Sources</u>: Apple, cabbage, carrots, cauliflower, citrus fruit, dried peas, green beans, potatoes, squash, and strawberries.

<u>Gums & Mucilages</u>: Perform functions similar to pectin.
*<u>Sources</u>: Oatmeal, rolled oats, kidney beans, pinto beans, lima beans, red beans, white beans, black beans, garbonzos, guar gum.
(Mucilages are sunflower and sesame seeds.)*

<u>Lignin</u>: Found in cell walls of plants, part of dietary fiber.
<u>Sources</u>: Pears, radishes, strawberries, green beans, eggplant.

<u>Cellulose</u>: Indigestible "bulk" which reduces constipation.
<u>Sources</u>: Whole wheat flour, bran, cabbage, young peas, green beans, wax beans, broccoli, brussel sprouts, cucumber skins, peppers, apples, carrots.

<u>Hemicellulose</u>: Holds water and produces bulk.
<u>Sources</u>: Bran, cereals, whole grains, beet root, mustard greens, brussel sprouts.

SOLUBLE FIBERS

Decreases cholesterol and triglycerides

1. *Protects against colon cancer*
2. *Helps to control blood pressure, blood sugar*
3. *Reduces constipation.*

INSOLUBLE FIBERS

Protects against toxic drugs, food additives, and chemicals

Protects against:
1. *colon cancer*
2. *constipation*
3. *diverticulitis*
4. *hemorrhoids*
5. *colitis*

HIGH FIBER FOODS

FOOD	SERVING	TOTAL FIBER
Oatmeal	1 Cup	3.5 Grams
Shredded Wheat	2 Biscuits	5.5 Grams
Oat Bran Cereal	1 Cup	7.5 Grams
100% Bran Cereal	1/3 Cup	8.5 Grams
Apple	1/2 Large	2 Grams
Pear	1 Medium	4 Grams
Strawberries	1 Cup	3 Grams
Kidney Beans	1/2 Cup	9.5 Grams
Sweet Corn	1/2 Cup	4.5 Grams
White Potato	1 Medium	4 Grams
Brown Rice	1 Cup	5 Grams
English Peas	1/2 Cup	6 Grams
Spinach	1/2 Cup	6.5 Grams
Carrots	1/2 Cup	3 Grams
Broccoli	1/2 Cup	3 Grams
Brussel Sprouts	1/2 Cup	6 Grams
Peas	1/2 Cup	6 Grams
Whole Wheat Bread	1 Slice	2 Grams
Nuts, (Pecans, Peanuts, Walnuts, Almonds)	10-12	2 Grams

VITAMINS AND MINERALS

Vitamins and minerals are required by the body to function normally. Vitamins and mineral supplements are popular in today's society; however, few of us need additional supplements if we eat properly. In our clinic, we have seen far more side effects from taking megadoses of vitamins and minerals than deficiencies from the lack of them. There is no evidence for the claim that natural vitamins are superior over synthetic vitamins. Evidence has shown megadoses of some B vitamins can often stimulate appetite.

Vitamin C:

* No evidence it is effective against cancer.
* May produce some symptomatic relief against colds.

(Consult your physician)

Vitamin E:

* No evidence it is useful in preventing aging, improving sexual function, treating muscular dystrophy, or heart disease.
* Megadoses of E can increase lipids which increase your risk of heart disease.
* Fibrocystic disease, lung damage and circulatory conditions may have some benefit from Vitamin E.

(Consult your physician)

The two (2) types of vitamins are fat soluble and water soluble. The fat soluble vitamins are stored in the body; therefore, the body does not excrete the excess. If amounts are stored in the system, soon side effects occur, many times resembling deficiency symptoms. Water soluble vitamins were at one time thought to be excreted from the body when excess amounts were consumed. New research has indicated this is not always true. Many of the water soluble vitamins may also remain in the body. At this time, there is little scientific data concerning vitamins and minerals. Remember, vitamins and minerals should be used with caution and are considered a chemical. The U. S. Recommended Daily Allowances are standards set up for an acceptable range of vitamins and minerals.

In the future, we will probably see the use of vitamins and minerals in treating many diseases. Some situations that require supplementation are:

Fad Dieters
Alcoholics
Person with Chronic Depression
Person with Stomach & Intestinal Disorders
Infants
Toddlers
Pregnant Women

Even in these situations, follow the recommendations of your physician or dietitian/nutritionist. In our clinic, we often recommend the use of a multivitamin/mineral supplement when participating in a weight loss program or if eating patterns fall short of the RDA's. Hopefully, most clients will lose weight and establish good eating habits, no longer requiring vitamin/mineral supplements. Remember, vitamins do not supply energy or calories to the body.

In the south, we tend to overcook our vegetables, losing water soluble vitamins. Fat soluble vitamins in foods are fairly stable; however, water soluble vitamins are easily destroyed. To avoid vitamin loss in foods:

1) Avoid excessively high temperatures in cooking.
2) Use a minimum amount of water in cooking.
3) Avoid excessive washing and dicing of foods.
4) Avoid excessive exposure to light.
5) Avoid prolonged storage time which affects the potency of many vitamins.

The requirements for minerals vary greatly. Calcium is the most abundant mineral in the body. After menopause, women require as much as 1500 milligrams to prevent brittle bone thinning, the disease called osteoporosis. The hormone estrogen aids in maintaining bone density by increasing calcium absorption. Be aware of your calcium needs before menopause. Statistics show individuals should build bone mass early in life with the proper amount of calcium (usually until about the age 35).

Once the loss starts occurring, very little can be done to slow the process. Exercise strengthens bones and spares calcium loss. Don't drink alcohol excessively or smoke. These risk factors have been shown to increase calcium loss.

There are many calcium supplements on the market. A supplement such as calcium carbonate has the highest rate of absorption (40%). Hormone therapy and calcium supplementation are often combined for maximum benefits; however, this should not totally replace calcium in the diet. We should still incorporate calcium rich foods in the diet.

CALCIUM RICH FOODS

Foods Equal to 1 Glass (8 oz.) Milk:

1/2 oz .cheddar cheese
2 cups cottage cheese
1 cup yogurt
1 1/2 cups ice milk
2 cups broccoli
1 cup collard or turnip greens.
4 oz. salmon

Salt is composed of two minerals-40% sodium and 50% chloride. Sodium is needed to maintain water balance and volume, along with normal nerve and muscle activity in the body. The body requires approximately 200 mg of sodium a day which can easily be met without adding any additional salt to foods or water.

Sodium requirements may vary depending on age, temperature, humidity, and level of activity.

The three to four grams recommended level for sodium per day is approximately 3,000-4,000 mg. In some people, too much salt causes high levels of fluid retention leading to high blood pressure.

Even untrained athletes can replace this minimal sodium loss during exercise by the normal food supply. Salt tablets are usually not necessary. In fact, salt tablets may cause dehydration by pulling water from the tissues to the stomach to dilute the sodium concentration. Usually additional fluids are needed rather than extra salt.

Remember, most foods naturally contain some sodium. Processed foods are the major sources of sodium. If you are on a strict low sodium diet, be sure to check the sodium content of your water by calling your local utilities. Many medications are high in sodium. The section on salt will reveal more on hidden sources on sodium.

AICR Guide to Vitamins

Vitamin (U.S. RDA)	Best Sources	Functions	Deficiency Symptoms
A Carotene (5,000 IU)	Liver, eggs, yellow & green fruits and vegetables, milk & dairy products, fish liver oil	Growth & repair of body tissues (resist infection), bone & tooth formation, visual purple production (necessary for night vision)	Night blindness, dry, scaly skin, loss of smell & appetite, susceptibility to infection, frequent fatigue, tooth decay
B₁ Thiamin (1.5 mg)	Wheat germ, yeast, liver, whole grains, nuts, fish, poultry, beans, meat	Carbohydrate metabolism, appetite maintenance, nerve function, growth & muscle tone	Heart irregularity, nerve disorders, fatigue, loss of appetite, forgetfulness
B₂ Riboflavin (1.7 mg)	Whole grains, green leafy vegetables, organ meats	Necessary for fat, carbohydrate, & protein metabolism, cell respiration, formation of antibodies & red blood cells	Eye problems, cracks in corners of mouth, digestive disturbances
B₆ Pyridoxine (2.0 mg)	Fish, poultry, lean meats	Necessary for fat, carbohydrate & protein metabolism, formation of antibodies, maintains sodium/potassium balance (nerves)	Nervousness, dermatitis, blood disorders, muscular weakness, insulin sensitivity, skin cracks, anemia
B₁₂ Cobalamin (6 mcg)	Organ meats, eggs, milk, fish, cheese	Carbohydrate, fat, protein metabolism, maintains healthy nervous system, blood cell formation	Pernicious anemia, nervousness, neuritis, fatigue, brain degeneration
Biotin (300 mcg)	Yeast, organ meats, legumes, eggs	Carbohydrate, fat, and protein metabolism, formation of fatty acids, helps utilize B vitamins	Dry, grayish skin, depression, muscle pain, fatigue, poor appetite
Choline (No RDA)	Organ meats, soybeans, fish, wheat germ, egg yolk	Nerve transmission, metabolism of fats & cholesterol, regulates liver & gall bladder	High blood pressure, bleeding stomach ulcers, liver & kidney problems
Folic Acid Folacin (400 mcg)	Green leafy vegetables, organ meats, milk products	Red blood cell formation, protein metabolism, growth & cell division	Anemia, gastrointestinal troubles, poor growth
Niacin (20 mg)	Meat, poultry, fish, milk products, peanuts, brewer's yeast	Fat, carbohydrate & protein metabolism, health of skin, tongue & digestive system, blood circulation	General fatigue, indigestion, irritability, loss of appetite, skin disorders
Pantothenic Acid (10 mg)	Lean meats, whole grains, legumes	Converts nutrients into energy, formation of some fats, vitamin utilization	Vomiting, stomach stress, restlessness, infections, muscle cramps
C Ascorbic Acid (60 mg)	Citrus fruits, vegetables, tomatoes, potatoes	Helps heal wounds, strength to blood vessels, collagen maintenance, resistance to infection	Bleeding gums, slow healing wounds, bruising, aching joints, nosebleeds, poor digestion
D (400 IU)	Fish-liver oils, egg yolks, organ meats, fish, fortified milk	Calcium & phosphorus metabolism (bone formation), heart action, nervous system maintenance	Rickets, poor bone growth, nervous system irritability
E (30 IU)	Vegetable oils, green vegetables, wheat germ, organ meats, eggs	Protects red blood cells, inhibits coagulation of blood, protects fat soluble vitamins, cellular respiration	Muscular wasting, abnormal fat deposits in muscles, gastrointestinal disease, heart disease

American Institute for Cancer Research • Washington, D.C. 20069

Reprinted with permission from the American Institute for Cancer Research.

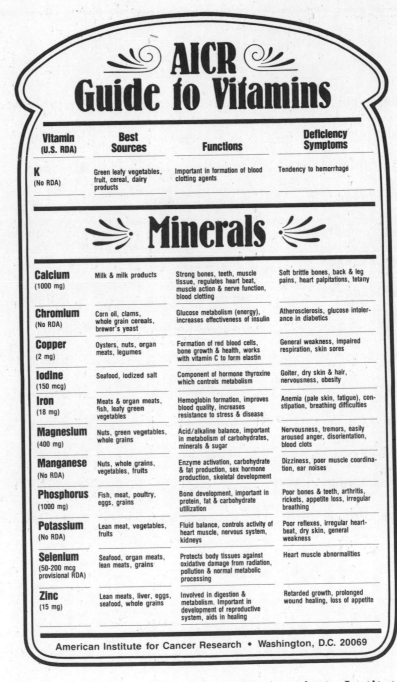

AICR Guide to Vitamins

Vitamin (U.S. RDA)	Best Sources	Functions	Deficiency Symptoms
K (No RDA)	Green leafy vegetables, fruit, cereal, dairy products	Important in formation of blood clotting agents	Tendency to hemorrhage

Minerals

	Best Sources	Functions	Deficiency Symptoms
Calcium (1000 mg)	Milk & milk products	Strong bones, teeth, muscle tissue, regulates heart beat, muscle action & nerve function, blood clotting	Soft brittle bones, back & leg pains, heart palpitations, tetany
Chromium (No RDA)	Corn oil, clams, whole grain cereals, brewer's yeast	Glucose metabolism (energy), increases effectiveness of insulin	Atherosclerosis, glucose intolerance in diabetics
Copper (2 mg)	Oysters, nuts, organ meats, legumes	Formation of red blood cells, bone growth & health, works with vitamin C to form elastin	General weakness, impaired respiration, skin sores
Iodine (150 mcg)	Seafood, iodized salt	Component of hormone thyroxine which controls metabolism	Goiter, dry skin & hair, nervousness, obesity
Iron (18 mg)	Meats & organ meats, fish, leafy green vegetables	Hemoglobin formation, improves blood quality, increases resistance to stress & disease	Anemia (pale skin, fatigue), constipation, breathing difficulties
Magnesium (400 mg)	Nuts, green vegetables, whole grains	Acid/alkaline balance, important in metabolism of carbohydrates, minerals & sugar	Nervousness, tremors, easily aroused anger, disorientation, blood clots
Manganese (No RDA)	Nuts, whole grains, vegetables, fruits	Enzyme activation, carbohydrate & fat production, sex hormone production, skeletal development	Dizziness, poor muscle coordination, ear noises
Phosphorus (1000 mg)	Fish, meat, poultry, eggs, grains	Bone development, important in protein, fat & carbohydrate utilization	Poor bones & teeth, arthritis, rickets, appetite loss, irregular breathing
Potassium (No RDA)	Lean meat, vegetables, fruits	Fluid balance, controls activity of heart muscle, nervous system, kidneys	Poor reflexes, irregular heartbeat, dry skin, general weakness
Selenium (50-200 mcg provisional RDA)	Seafood, organ meats, lean meats, grains	Protects body tissues against oxidative damage from radiation, pollution & normal metabolic processing	Heart muscle abnormalities
Zinc (15 mg)	Lean meats, liver, eggs, seafood, whole grains	Involved in digestion & metabolism. Important in development of reproductive system, aids in healing	Retarded growth, prolonged wound healing, loss of appetite

American Institute for Cancer Research • Washington, D.C. 20069

Reprinted with permission from the American Institute for Cancer Research.

EQUIVALENTS

3 teaspoons	....	1 tablespoon
4 teaspoons	....	1/4 cup
5 1/3 tablespoons	....	1/3 cup
8 tablespoons	....	1/2 cup
10 2/3 tablespoons	....	2/3 cup
12 tablespoons	....	3/4 cup
16 tablespoons	....	1 cup
2 cups	....	1 pint
4 cups	....	1 quart
4 quarts	....	1 gallon
16 ounces	....	1 pound
32 ounces	....	1 quart
8 ounces liquid	....	1 cup
1 ounce liquid	....	2 tablespoons

INGREDIENT SUBSTITUTES

1 tablespoon corn starch   EQUALS   2 tablespoons flour
or
4 teaspoons tapioca

1 cup buttermilk   EQUALS   1 tablespoon lemon
or
vinegar plus sweet milk to make 1 cup

1 tablespoon fresh herbs   EQUALS   1 teaspoon dried herbs

1 small fresh onion   EQUALS   1 tablespoon instant minced onion

1 teaspoon dry mustard   EQUALS   1 tablespoon prepared mustard

1 cup tomato juice   EQUALS   1/2 cup tomato sauce plus 1/2 cup water

3 tablespoons cocoa plus
1 tablespoon oil   EQUALS   1 square unsweetened chocolate

1 whole egg   EQUALS   2 egg whites or 1/4 cup egg substitute

INDEX BY FOOD GROUPS

COOKIES

DESSERTS

DINNERS

DIPS AND DRESSINGS

FISH